PROFIT AT ANY COST?

WHY BUSINESS ETHICS MAKES SENSE

JERRY FLEMING

Baker Books

A Division of Baker Book House Co
Grand Rapids, Michigan 49516

Published by Baker Books
a division of Baker Book House Company
P.O. Box 6287, Grand Rapids, MI 49516-6287
www.bakerbooks.com

Printed in the United States of America

Library of Congress Cataloging-in-Publication Data
Fleming, Jerry, 1939–
    Profit at any cost? : why business ethics makes sense / Jerry Fleming.
        p.   cm.
    ISBN 0-8010-1259-7
    1. Business ethics. I Title.
    HF5387 .F58 2003
    174' .4—dc21   2002154566

CONTENTS

Acknowledgments

Many people have contributed to the writing of this book. My sincere gratitude to the following people, who made a direct contribution, for their guidance and counsel:

- Jim Bender, Director of Ethics and Corporate Compliance Programs of Texas Instruments, for providing feedback on the relevance of the material to the real world of business. He gave his time, without compensation, because he felt strongly about this issue and wanted to maximize the book's impact.
- Lisa C. Crocker, concept advisor, whose tactful counsel enabled me to make the necessary changes to improve the book's professionalism and readability while retaining my ego.
- Dr. George Davis, my friend, for his encouragement to take on this endeavor. Without it, I probably wouldn't have written this book.
- Pepper Fleming, my son and a dotcom executive, who kept me from preaching to the academic chair.

He helped me focus on communicating with people who have to live with these issues in the business world.

- Sonin Fleming, my wife, who deserves a medal. It was her sacrifice that facilitated this undertaking. Without her patience, understanding, and encouragement, I could not have kept my butt in my chair long enough to finish.
- Mary Jane Havens, an executive, for being a sounding board for how specific issues are presented.
- Randy Kozak for providing a buffer between the day-to-day issues of running my company and myself. He afforded me the time and freedom to write.
- Dr. John McDermit, scientist, businessman, and friend, who has been a source of counsel throughout this undertaking. His assistance in getting through some rough spots has made a significant difference in the presentation of this material.
- Elizabeth Fleming McDougal, my daughter, for providing freshness to what could be a stale subject.
- Susan Titus Osborn, for editing but also for going beyond editing and providing insight into how to make the material interesting and engaging.
- Bill Petersen, Senior Editor of Baker Book House, for believing in the need for this book and for publishing it.

Thank you.

INTRODUCTION

Why in the world would I consider writing a book on business ethics when there have already been good books written on the subject? In fact, I'm looking at one right now. And guess what the title is? *Business Ethics,* by Herbert Johnson. I know this subject has been covered by a number of business professionals and philosophers, most of whom know a lot more about the subject than I. This issue has been dissected more ways than a preacher can ask for money. I do, however, have one advantage over most of these people: I've been there, done that, and got the T-shirt. I've been on both sides of the issue and have seen the results of doing right *and* of doing wrong. Therefore, I have the perspective of viewing this issue from both sides. The best way I know to entice you to read this book and to explain my motivation for writing it is to tell you about the experience that planted the seed.

For some time I have wanted to investigate whether a relationship exists between business and morality. Born during the depression, I was taught two things: First, to do right. Second, to be successful, which included mak-

ing money. Throughout my business career, I was in conflict over these issues and wondered if these two philosophies were compatible.

In 1992, a mild heart attack provided just the nudge
I needed to investigate this issue seriously. We all have
things we want to do someday; well, for me, "someday"
had arrived. I decided to retire from the day-to-day operations of running the company I had founded years earlier and go back to school and study this apparent
paradox.

Dr. Hal Hadden, a friend of mine, told me of a unique
program offered by Oxford Graduate School (an affili-
ate of Oxford University, England) in Dayton, Tennessee.
Upon investigation, I discovered the school offered a doctorate in Religion and Society, a research degree that
applies Christian principles to secular activities. I decided that this program was just what I was looking for.
Now I would have the tools to help me explore the issue
that had intrigued me for years: the relationship between
business and morality.

One year into the program, the school discovered that
I had not satisfied the language requirement, which was
a prerequisite for their program. Of course, I knew I
hadn't taken a foreign language; I was happy just semi-
mastering English. Well, I tried every excuse I knew, but
the school was adamant. It looked like I was going to
have to go back to undergraduate school to take twelve
hours of a foreign language.

There was no way! There had to be some way out of
this dilemma. After seeing me fret and moan about this
until she couldn't stand it anymore, my wife, Sonin, came
up with an ingenious solution. She said, "Jerry, you have
mentioned several times that you would like to study
Spanish in a Spanish-speaking country. Why don't you
kill two birds with one stone? Let's go to Mexico and take
one of those total-immersion Spanish courses."

Of course, I was sure Oxford would never approve it. It sounded like too much fun. Much to my astonishment, Oxford accepted this program "provided it was through an accredited university and satisfied the school's scholastic requirements." Sonin, the research queen, went to work and found the perfect university program in Puerto Vallarta, Mexico.

The next project was to locate a place to stay while taking the course. We didn't want to stay in an American hotel where we would be able to speak English, so, after days of research, Sonin once again came up with what seemed the perfect solution. The Casa de Maria, eight hundred feet above the city in the hills overlooking the sea, seemed ideal.

According to the brochure, the bungalow was as spectacular as the scenery. The Spanish décor, both inside and outside the casa, looked beautiful, and the patio came with a hot tub and a sunset view. As an added plus, the Casa de Maria was located in a lovely, old section of town. Sonin noted, "There's probably not an American within ten miles, so if you don't speak Spanish, you don't speak."

I was ecstatic. We were going to be totally immersed in old Mexico. I was already visualizing us sitting in the hot tub, watching the sunset, and speaking Spanish while listening to mariachi music coming from the city below. Definitely the way God intended that school should be.

We left Nashville, Tennessee, on a cold and rainy February morning. We arrived in Puerto Vallarta about three o'clock on an Africa-hot afternoon. As soon as we landed, events began easing me out of my hot-tub fantasies and back into my usual "Captain Doom" mode. Instead of taxiing to the terminal, the plane stopped about one-quarter of a mile away, and we waited half an hour in the sweltering heat for buses to come and take us the rest of the way. Finally, a pair of buses that looked as though they were from the movie *Romancing the Stone* lumbered up to the plane. At this point, I began to question the wisdom of this trip. However, Sonin, always the voice of optimism, said, "Don't go Captain Doom on me. In an hour we'll be in our beautiful casa, sitting in our hot tub, watching the sunset, and listening to mariachi music."

We loaded our considerable "stuff" onto the bus, which had no air-conditioning, rode to the terminal, and unloaded. Then we waited in the interminable customs line. Finally, we were cleared and found ourselves a *taxista* (cab driver). Although Sonin and I had been studying Spanish tapes together (being of Latin descent she was light-years ahead of me in learning the language), we couldn't speak enough Spanish, and the *taxista* couldn't speak enough English to carry on a conversation. As a result, our communication was limited to "Casa de Maria, *por favor*" (please) and "*cuanto cuesta*" (how much).

We loaded the trunk and most of the back seat, then climbed in, and headed for the city. It was just what we had hoped for—very Spanish and very clean. The red-tile-roofed, stucco buildings were in good repair. The cobblestone streets were lined with palm trees, the people were clean and well dressed, and the city had a pleasant, tropical, and almost festive atmosphere. Beyond the city, we could see mountains, lush and green with foliage, rising right out of the Pacific Ocean. What a sight! It really did look like a brochure from a travel agency. As we drove along the *malecon* (boardwalk) beside the ocean, I began to relax, thinking, "We made the right decision. This will be an adventure."

After about thirty minutes of beautiful scenery, the cab abruptly turned left and started up a steep mountain. With the car in low gear and the tires spinning, we inched upward at a rate of about one mile per hour through a cobblestone *aliado* (alley) so steep I doubt if an American mule could climb it. As we ascended, the houses got smaller, closer together, and more dilapidated.

When we finally reached the top, the cab took a right turn and drove through an even smaller *aliado*, which opened into a cobblestone bluff. At the edge of this bluff was a fifty-foot drop with no guardrail and no warning signs. To the left of the cliff, there was a group of stucco hovels that looked like a series of porches—stacks of rooms with the front wall missing. The opening where the front wall should have been was covered with either a bamboo roman shade or shutters. Some of the hovels had waist-high walls across the front with broken bottles glued to them to prevent undesirables from climbing in. Others had steel bars covering the front opening.

The cab driver got out, pointed to the hovels, and announced, "Casa de Maria."

After I caught my breath, I said in my best Spanish, "No, amigo, no Casa de Maria."

He replied with a big grin, "Si, señor, Casa de Maria."

Sonin, the voice of reason, asked him to wait while we checked.

Well, there was no Maria anywhere, only a key with a note attached that read, *"Bienvenido, el Flemings, vosotros estas casa numero seis."* This meant we were in the right place, and we had hovel number six. Investigating, we discovered that the hovel's interior matched its exterior and also provided a few more interesting surprises. The single room was partitioned into two sections. The good news was that we had running water and a bathroom. The bad news was that the bathroom (a tub and a commode) was in the bedroom and only a thin partition away from the living and dining area.

Needless to say, neither hovel number six nor Casa de Maria was what we had expected. Where were the beau-

13

tiful ornate buildings, the lovely patio, and the hot tub? Where was the air-conditioning? We reviewed the situation: we had paid in advance, it was now getting dark, we were tired, and we had no place to go. Sonin, the eternal optimist, said, "Look at the bright side; the view's nice and *our* hovel has shutters and bars!" Reluctantly, we decided to stay the night and kill Maria in the morning.

Finding her proved difficult. We invested several days in trying to track her down, during which time our Casa de Maria experience fell far short of the idyll promised by the glossy brochure. Instead of sitting in our hot tub, watching the sunset and listening to mariachi music, we were adjusting to primitive conditions, without the modern conveniences we had previously taken for granted. Although Sonin had turned the place into the nicest hovel in the area, we just couldn't get used to people speaking to us from the street while we were lying in bed or taking a bath. We Americans are funny that way. After a few days, we reluctantly gave up our deposit and sought more suitable accommodations. We never were able to find Maria.

The Point of the Story

Maria was unethical. She misled us with a brochure and information that completely misrepresented the accommodations she provided. Being in Mexico, a foreign country, we believed we had no recourse. We felt cheated and resentful. The Casa de Maria portion of our trip was a bad experience.

But Maria was also shortsighted. Although she made a small profit from us, her unethical behavior cost her money in the long run. We have returned to Mexico twice since this experience, and we have many friends who travel regularly to Puerto Vallarta. Had Maria been honest with us, we would not have stayed in such primitive accommodations. However, we have friends who enjoy that kind of experience, and we could have sent her more business. Instead, she has lost business because Sonin and I have advised our friends to avoid Casa de Maria. Also, while we were there, we became friends with a man who owns an accommodations rental company. Guess where he *doesn't* send his clients? Our dissatisfaction really helped to shorten the Casa de Maria's potential guest list.

This experience planted the seeds for this book. After returning from Mexico and pondering the amount of business Maria lost because of her deceptive advertising, I decided, for my dissertation, to investigate the relationship between being ethical (or unethical) and being profitable to see if this relationship could be scientifically correlated. *Profit at Any Cost?* is the result of that research.

PART 1

THE SLIPPERY SLOPE

In the time of the greatest economic growth in history, we seem to have sunk to the lowest ethical level in our national experience.

William Lawrence

1

ENRON

The Tip of the Iceberg?

Selecting the site was a no brainer. Naples, Florida, in April is about as good as it gets. It's between tourist seasons. Yet the weather is still cool enough to enjoy walks on the beach, and the sunsets are spectacular. The hotel was also a given—a meeting of this importance deserved to be in the best—the Palms. Not only was its elegance and charm unmatched in southwest Florida, but also it was off the beaten path. There would be little chance of running into friends or future competitors.

The meeting was instigated and arranged by the chairman of Natural Gas & Oil Distribution Inc. (NG&O) for Friday, 2:00 P.M. NG&O was located outside of Dallas, Texas. The company purchased and resold oil and natural gas and also owned a small exploration company that concentrated in the Oklahoma Anadarko basin. The chairman was in his midfifties, medium height and build, full gray hair, and glasses that complemented a pleasant face. It would take only seconds to realize he was educated, articulate, and well mannered.

He had invited three other men, and to make this work, he would need all three on board. A table had been reserved in a private dining room with a large window overlooking the bay. He felt they would attract little attention. Even if someone they knew came in, they probably wouldn't be noticed, much less recognized.

The second person to arrive was the third best energy trader in the country. Why wasn't the best chosen? Because of this guy's intelligence, ego, and his reputation for making deals—one way or another. He was in his early forties, tall, black hair thinning in front, wiry, with a ruddy complexion. Although he was from the poor side of the Bronx, he had learned to modify his persona to fit the occasion . . . and the client. Only when he was stressed for a long period did his backstreet mannerisms begin to emerge.

The chairman stood up and shook hands, "Would you like something to drink?" he asked.

"Yes, I need a martini . . . dry. Man, I can't believe that even Florida can be this hot in April," the trader replied.

As if on cue, the third member of the meeting showed up. He was an auditor from one of the big five accounting firms. The man had been the lead auditor at NG&O for the past five years. In his late forties, he had blond hair thinning into pattern baldness. He was six-one and weighed about two hundred pounds. Typical build. The chairman had chosen him because the last three years, he had allowed profits to be inflated through overstating the value of inventories and other assets at NG&O. Also, he had confided that he had been passed over for promotion, and he was about ready to jump ship and make some real money.

As they were shaking hands, a pretty young lady in a well-tailored, short dress appeared and asked, "Would you gentleman like to order something to drink?"

The energy trader turned, took a long look, and asked, "Where were you when I needed you last night?" Taken aback, the waitress was about to respond when the chairman interrupted, noticing the fourth and last of the foursome walking toward the table.

The fourth man was the linchpin to the plan—the financier, the moneyman. Midforties, black wavy hair, brawny, six-two, and over 220 pounds, he was the guy who would put together an equity offering and convince a select group of investors of the success of the new venture and a rate of return that would rival illegal drugs—but without the risk. Although he needed no introduction, the chairman introduced him to the rest of the men.

Then, to the relief of the young lady, the chairman confirmed everyone's drink and ordered. After a pause, he added, "And bring us a bottle of your best wine with our meal—something that goes well with southwest Florida fish and new friends."

After the waitress crossed the room and walked out the door, they sat down. The financier was about to say how cute the waitress was when another waiter rounded the table, poured water, placed napkins in everyone's lap and menus in each one's hand. Then he disappeared.

Instead of continuing remarks at the waitress's expense, the trader turned to the chairman and asked, "What's this about?"

The chairman thought for a moment and responded, "I think you will be pleased with what I'm going to propose, but I would like to wait until we order and can give our full attention to the discussion."

The trader rubbed his chin and leaned back. "If you want my attention, we better change waitresses."

After the laughter died down, the chairman said with a chuckle, "Don't worry, she only takes bar orders." At that, everyone sighed and picked up their menus.

After lengthy discussions with a new waiter about which southwest Florida fish would be best this time of year, negotiating over special requests, and emphasizing the importance of cooking at the right temperature and the exact length of time, the men placed their orders. Attention finally turned to the purpose of their "get-to-gather," as the chairman called it.

"Gentlemen," the chairman said, "I propose to make all of you very rich within a reasonably short period of time, allowing you to live a wealthy lifestyle while you are getting there."

The financier looked at him with a grin, "Hey, I'm already rich—but I can always use more money."

To which the chairman responded, "Hold on, I'm talking big money—maybe billions."

There was silence. The auditor looked at the financier and the trader and nodded his head. "Listen to him, gentlemen. He knows what he's talking about."

The financier took a sip of his martini. "Okay, you've got my attention. What have you got in mind? But, I'll tell you up front, this better be good; I've already got some deals cooking that will use up most of my influence capital, not to mention my clients' money."

The chairman held up his hands in a gesture for attention. "Okay, let's get to it. Here it is in a nutshell. NG&O is for sale. I propose we create a new corporation called Energy Corporation of America (ECA) and sell stock to capitalize it to a select group of clients who understands this sort of thing. Our 'whiz kid' financier here, using some special accounting rules discovered by our creative accountant, will inflate the value of the assets and develop a long-range plan to convince our investors to provide funding for the purchase and a sinful amount of working capital. Our 'independent' but friendly auditor here will, of course, bless all of this through his accounting firm.

"After the acquisition, we create a trading division to be headed up by our trader who will, after making enough legitimate deals to establish credibility, also indulge in some creative accounting. He will establish partnerships in other countries that will make slightly irregular energy deals between them as needed to show healthy profits and move the 'paper' as necessary. This will hide the debt and keep it off the books and will allow ECA to show sufficient profit to grow the stock (of which we will have a healthy share) in value very quickly. This in turn will allow ECA to issue more stock to provide additional funding for expansion."

The trader then asked, "I don't understand how this can get by the SEC."

"It's not as hard as you think," replied the auditor. "The rules governing what has to be disclosed are so convoluted that if you produce the right section that covers that particular transaction, it's accepted. Remember, you aren't defending the partnerships at that time, only ECA. If the SEC wants to see a particular partnership's books, when they give notice, 'sell' the paper to another one."

The trader shook his head. "I can't believe this will work. Even if the SEC can be fooled, the stock markets aren't that naive. What happens if we are exposed?"

To this the chairman laughed, "If we see it coming, we simply sell our stock, make a bundle of money, and take the fifth. Remember, we will be viewed as the fair-haired boys trying to free America of its dependence on foreign energy. The gas-hungry public will understand. As long as fuel is available and reasonably priced, they

23

will turn a deaf ear to risky ventures and unorthodox methodology. You know, God, mother, apple pie, and all that. And there's no doubt the politicians will bend toward public perception."

"Also," added the auditor, "it's being done as we speak and by several companies using basically the same techniques."

Actually, It's a Slippery Slope

Things don't generally start out this way, do they? But the power of the above story is in its illustration. Things look ridiculous when they are condensed to their essence and exposed to the light without the incremental development of subtle events over time to influence our opinions.

Generally, moving away from good intentions to create something healthy for everybody is a slow progression. Then there is a problem that requires a creative solution. And sooner or later, another problem, same type of fix, and on and on. It's a slippery slope. Before we realize it, we are deeply involved in doing things we never thought we would do. Without a value system to keep us from making those seemingly insignificant choices that start us down the wrong path, we have no signposts to tell us when we are turning the wrong way.

In the case of Enron, there are no indications that either Enron's or Andersen's involvement in the present scandal was hatched at a series of clandestine meetings by a cast of unsavory characters, as the above story portrays.

Enron was created as the result of a 1985 merger between two well-established natural gas companies: Houston Natural Gas (HNG) and InterNorth, a Nebraska-based natural gas pipeline company. The new company was formed to make money—for sure—but also in the process to decrease America's dependence on foreign energy. And it was based on a sound value system, designed to keep the company honest and ethical.

Enron's Value System

RESPECT	COMMUNICATION
We treat others as we would like to be treated ourselves. We do not tolerate abusive or disrespectful treatment. Ruthlessness, callousness and arrogance don't belong here.	We have an obligation to communicate. Here, we take the time to talk with one another . . . and to listen. We believe that information is meant to move and that information moves people.
INTEGRITY	EXCELLENCE
We work with customers and prospects openly, honestly and sincerely. When we say we will do something, we will do it; when we say we cannot or will not do something, then we won't do it.	We are satisfied with nothing less than the very best in everything we do. We will continue to raise the bar for everyone. The great fun here will be for all of us to discover just how good we can really be.

Source: Enron.com/investors resources/annual report 1998, http://www.enron.com/corp/investors/annuals/annual98

Kenneth Lay, a Ph.D. in economics and a former Exxon executive, was the chief executive officer of HNG. The company focused its attention on developing its natural gas interests. While in that position, he was successful in creating the nation's only transcontinental gas pipeline. And when Enron was formed, Dr. Lay was to become CEO of the new company.

In the beginning, the new company seemed to honestly focus on this value system and on developing its people. In an interview with *Business 2.0*, middle manager Fred Philipson, even after being forced to move on, said, "Trouble is, there is no place (I would) rather be. They . . . molded me and gave me chances to do creative things."[1]

As long as Enron focused on producing and transmitting energy, the company seemed to adhere to the value system it espoused. It appears that when management decided to diversify into trading energy futures and bundling services for specific customers in 1986, its values started to change.

As I said earlier, these things don't happen overnight. According to an October 1985 *Vanity Fair* article, a New York bank notified an Enron audit executive that money was being transferred from Enron Oil, a subsidiary of Enron, to personal accounts. The ensuing investigation by internal personnel confirmed this, but the perpetrators who made the transfers were able to give "plausible" explanations (after they were caught) as to why they had done it.

Nothing was done. One source believes it was because of the apparent profits being created, in the $500 million range, from this division. They were afraid they would kill the goose that was laying the golden egg. Much later, it was discovered that, like other divisions, the profits were nonexistent.[2]

The real lesson learned from this experience was that with a little creative accounting and maneuvering dramatic profits could be shown that would drive up the price of the stock and attract more investors. In the twelve years that followed, Enron became very creative in finding ways to increase profits. They sold overvalued assets and moved more into the seemingly profitable energy trading, which necessitated developing more and more partnerships to keep mounting debt off Enron's balance sheet. Also, they swapped control of fiber data lines with those of another company, only to undo the transaction a few days later to create the appearance of volume. By the midnineties, Enron had also become sophisticated in their SEC accounting. They had found ways around reporting stock transactions in partnerships as required.[3]

The final chapter of this story hasn't been written yet, but at this point, we know at least that smoke and mirrors were used to finance growth and line management's pockets. But in the final analysis, regardless of where the money or debt is hidden, it's still green—or red.

Interestingly, another change in Enron's value system evolved with their creative accounting. In their value statement, it says, "We treat others as we would like to be treated ourselves." The creative systems mentioned above were designed to inflate profits and value. This deceived investors and employees—both stockholders and debtors. Surely, they wouldn't have wanted to be treated that way.

Talk about the Wolf Watching the Henhouse!

For me, the primary issue is with the auditors. I believe Arthur Andersen started out with Enron with the same professionalism and objectivity all auditing firms have with their clients. The relationship began in 1993 when Andersen became the in-house auditor after the myriads of partnerships had been created to move money and debt off Enron's books. I suspect that with Enron being such a plum, the new auditors, wanting to make the association work, bent over backward to find legitimate ways to justify Enron's convoluted operating structure. Apparently, Enron was able to convince Andersen that the partnerships were legitimate, and the losses from Enron Oil were nonexistent or insignificant. In any event, no warnings were sounded outside of Enron management.[4]

In the years that followed, Andersen allowed Enron to overstate its profits by nearly $600 million and understate its debts by over a billion dollars. Ultimately this resulted in investors, employee-stockholders, and debtors losing billions in stock value.[5]

For its oversight (yes, a play on words), Andersen was compensated handsomely. In 2000 they earned $25 million in auditing fees and $27 million in consulting fees.[6]

I'm not an accountant, but I have been on the other end of many audits. Over the years, I have learned that auditors have to be careful to separate the auditing function from the consulting function to the point that one hand doesn't know what the other hand is doing. Anything less will influence the audit, which is supposed to be independent. It would be best if the same company did not provide both functions.

The role of an auditor of a publicly held company is to assess financial health and to disclose any potential problems that might adversely affect the company's future to all stakeholders.[7]

Two basic tenets of auditing are:

1. Value assets at the lower of cost or market.
2. Book profits after the transaction has been completed.

In the *Vanity Fair* article, an Enron lawyer still at the company described the moment when Enron's chief financial officer (CFO) introduced her to a concept of monetization in which future revenue is booked immediately. The nerve behind the logic baffled the lawyer. She told him, "It seems to me that if you do a 10-year deal, and suck all the earnings out in one year, you will then have to keep the profit coming though years 4, 5, 6, and all the way to 10, by doing more of these deals." It looked to the lawyer like a pyramid scheme, but she knew that the accounting department had signed off on it! The CFO replied, "Yes, you have to keep doing more of these deals each year."[8]

Andersen not only failed to meet their obligation to provide assurance that the financials were accurate but also didn't disclose a fair and impartial evaluation of the company's less-than-arm's-length financial dealings to its stakeholders and potential investors. In short, Andersen failed to do its job.

According to William Lerach of the law firm Milberg, Weiss, Bershad, Hynes, & Lerach, LLP, not only did sophisticated investors get burned, but retirement funds belonging to middle- and low-income people were lost. The University of California retirement system claimed a loss of $145 million and Florida claimed $335 million. The total loss to state pension funds was $2.9 billion.

CNN reported that in 2001 the Enron employees' 401K had 62 percent of its retirement funds of $1.3 billion invested in company stock. That would be about $800 million. I have not found any estimates of how much Enron's employees lost in the company's stock retirement program, but it most certainly was the bulk of some people's nest eggs.[9] According to Lerach, Enron's upper management fared better. Twenty-nine officials had sold their stock before the news hit the networks, for an estimated $1.1 billion.[10] Remember their value statement, "We treat others as we would like to be treated ourselves." Who does it apply to?

Enron may be only the tip of the iceberg. We know of other companies that have experienced some of the same accounting failures:

- October 1995: Bausch and Lomb overstated income by $17.6 million.
- November 1999: Rite Aid overstated revenue by $1 billion.
- December 1999: Cendant overstated income by $500 million.

29

- May 2001: Sunbeam was charged by the SEC for accounting fraud.
- June 2001: Waste Management overstated earnings by more than $1 billion between 1992 and 1996.[11]

And as this is being written the stock market is reeling in anticipation of more corruption surfacing in publicly held corporations:

- WorldCom, the communications giant, has announced it has overstated its profits by $3 billion over the past five quarters.
- Global Crossing, also a worldwide communications company, has filed for bankruptcy and is being investigated by the SEC and the House Financial Services Committee.
- Martha Stewart (no, not Martha Stewart!) is fighting to keep her domestic diva title. She is suspected of unlawfully selling ImClone stock after receiving insider information from the founder, her friend Sam Waksal.

The President Responds

In response to these disclosures, President Bush issued a statement, "Reform must begin with accountability, and that reform must start at the top." In order to protect America's shareholders, the administration developed a ten-point plan guided by three principles:

1. Provide better information to investors.
2. Make corporate officers more accountable.
3. Develop a stronger, more independent audit system.

The President's Ten-Point
Corporate Responsibility Plan

1. Each investor should have quarterly access to the information needed to judge a firm's financial performance, condition, and risks.
2. Each investor should have prompt access to critical information.
3. CEOs should personally vouch for the veracity, timeliness, and fairness of their companies' public disclosures, including their financial statements.
4. CEOs or other officers should not be allowed to profit from erroneous financial statements.
5. CEOs or other officers who clearly abuse their power should lose their right to serve in any corporate leadership position.
6. Corporate leaders should be required to tell the public promptly whenever they buy or sell company stock for personal gain.
7. Investors should have complete confidence in the independence and integrity of companies' auditors.
8. An independent regulatory board should ensure that the accounting profession is held to the highest ethical standards.
9. The authors of accounting standards must be responsive to the needs of investors.
10. Firms' accounting systems should be compared with best practices, not simply against minimum standards.[12]

Reform must begin with accountability, and that reform must start at the top.

President George W. Bush

It is obvious to me that there are many more companies out there that are using ingenious means of inflating profits and minimizing debt. I believe the president is right to take this stand for easier access to information. Unfortunately, we have more than enough rules and regulations now to provide guidance to those who want to be ethical. The problem is that even honest, hardworking people, who live out their moral beliefs in the workplace (and are now invested in the stock market), don't really believe that honesty and morality in the corporate office is the most profitable policy.

Summary

Remember the 2002 Winter Olympics? Although we were outraged by the bribe used to successfully secure the games for Salt Lake City and the allegations of unethical judging during them, now they are all but forgotten. Enron, Arthur Andersen, WorldCom, and Martha Stewart (isn't anything sacred?) have taken the spotlight, and our attention has been turned away from the Olympics' scandals to the drama of executives testifying at congressional hearings. Even though there were public outcries against all of these activities, will justice really be served? Or will yesterday's transgressions just continue to fade as new corruptions surface?

Until men and women in corporate management are willing to take a moral stand when things don't "smell" right, when something violates their sense of right and wrong, the modus operandi will not change. Until corporate America views manipulation and applying "fuzzy" logic to situations for personal gain as unacceptable, continuing to make new laws and regulations to cover new situations will not make any real difference.

How do we accomplish this? Read on.

2

IS THE SYSTEM FLAWED?

It's easier to fight for one's principles than to live up to them.

Mark Twain

D o you know anyone who said, "When I grow up, I want to be a ruthless, cunning, and deceitful business person?" It doesn't happen that way, does it? When you leave the academic world to make your mark, you expect to do good things—good for your-self and good for those you touch. You expect to make the world a better place.

After assuming a position of responsibility, it gener-ally doesn't take long for that bubble to burst. Soon you are confronted with an ethical situation where doing what is expected conflicts with doing what is right. You realize the roses you've been smelling are growing out of a pile of manure. That's what happened to me.

Because of hard work, a little luck, and knowing the right people, I left my familiar world of engineering for the glitzy world of corporate management. Instead of being permanently mired in a swamp of formulas and equations, I was elevated to the lofty position of chief operating officer (COO) of a thriving (so I thought) manufacturing company. Being an engineer isn't far removed from the academic world, because you are insulated from the pressures of having to make a profit in a hostile, competitive business environment. When I assumed my new command, I thought that running a business was like running a design project. If you collected the right data and plugged in the right formulas, you would get the right answers and—voilà, you would be successful!

My new company had been recently acquired by a holding company, and the chairman of my board— we'll call him *Ray*—was a principal in the parent corporation. The Human Resources Department had hired me, and I had only spoken with Ray, my new boss, a few times. I did, however, know him by reputation. He was known for achieving his goals regardless of the obstacles, and he had no use for people who didn't share this philosophy.

When Ray's secretary called, she simply said, "Mr. Smith would like for you to come to his office. Would two o'clock this afternoon be convenient?" Of course, I wasn't going to say "no," convenient or not! I did muster the courage to ask, "Do you know what this is regarding?" "No," she responded, "he didn't say."

I gathered all the materials I thought he might be interested in, threw them into a briefcase, and began the thirty-mile drive from my office to "the ivory tower," his office suite. I had just enough time to make it, if I exceeded the speed limit and the traffic was light. I was in luck—it was five minutes before two when I walked through the large glass doors of the "tower."

As I walked past the ornate receptionist's vestibule, I noticed a plaque behind the desk that read: "There is a way that seems right to the simple, but in the end the road leads to disaster." What a curious statement, I thought, as I entered the chairman's office and settled into one of his big comfortable wingback chairs. Had I been older and more experienced, I might have recognized the wisdom of the statement. But, I was young, focused, and . . . simple.

Ray offered me coffee, which I dutifully accepted, and after exchanging a few pleasantries, he stood, walked over to his window, and with his back to me said, "Jerry, you have a problem."

After pausing what seemed like at least five minutes, he went on. "We're involved in a product liability lawsuit that's threatening the company's very existence. Before you came on board, we had sued our competitors for infringing on our patents. I just got word that the judge ruled against us."

I knew a little of the background and that this meant we were paying royalties on patented products for which we had no protection. Looking as reflective as I knew how, I said, "Go on."

There is a way that seems right to the simple, but in the end the road leads to disaster.

Ray turned toward me and said, "We can't compete if we have to pay royalties on our products and the competition doesn't. There's just not enough profit in this industry." Then, he asked, "What do you propose we do about it?"

What do I propose we do about it? I was thirty-three years old, and as a manager still wet behind the ears! I'm sure it showed on my face as the thought crossed my mind, "Why in blazes didn't they tell me about this before I came on board?" Trying not to react negatively, I responded, "I'm missing something. Why should we have to pay royalties on patented products that we can't defend?"

I might have guessed; Ray was one step ahead of me. "I have already contacted the inventor and told him that if we lost this suit, we would stop paying the patent fees. The inventor's attorney responded that if we stopped payments, they would file suit against us. They contend the contract gives us permission to manufacture and sell the product in addition to giving us an exclusive on the patents. According to the attorney, we are obligated to pay royalties as long as we produce and sell the equipment."

We were in a no-win situation. I stood and tried to look as intelligent as I could. "Ray, I don't have any answers. What do you think we should do?"

Again, he was one step ahead of me. "One thing I've learned over the years is that you don't fight a war if there is nothing to win." As I was pondering the meaning of his war statement, he said, "They have asked to see the company's financial statement."

I realized that this wasn't good for our side. Before taking the job I had reviewed the financial statements, and I knew the company was fiscally strong.

Ray made a curious observation, "If the company were in bad shape financially, they probably would drop the suit or settle."

"Maybe," I said, "but our balance sheet is solid."

Ray took a sip of coffee and turned back toward the window. "Perhaps . . . we could get creative and do something to change that. We really need to settle this out of court."

At this point, I realized that Ray had already thought this through and was just bringing me along. Although I wasn't sure where he was going, something told me I wasn't going to like it.

When he realized I was too stupid or naive to catch on, he spelled it out for me in spades. "Before we give them the information, let's bankrupt the company."

"Bankrupt the company?" I asked.

In a condescending tone, he said, "Jerry, all we have to do is eliminate the company's equity."

My heart skipped a beat and I felt sick. I sat back down, took a deep breath, got control of my emotions, and forced myself not to react. "Yes, that would change the situation, wouldn't it?" I'm sure Ray saw my reaction, but he didn't show it. Instead, he began to explore ways this could be accomplished. For a while I just sat there trying to look engaged. Curiously, as he talked and discussed the possibilities, the sick feeling in my stomach went away. I began to view his proposal with detached objectivity.

In hindsight, I should have stood up and said, "Ray, this is deceitful and probably illegal. I can't do this." But I was the new COO. I was out to make my mark and eager to prove they had made a good choice. I was resolved to be the best chief executive they had ever had—even if it meant compromising my ethics. I was playing with the big boys now. I was running a business, and business has its own ethic, doesn't it? We spent the rest of the afternoon devising a plan to gut the company of its equity, and I spent the next week implementing it.

The Rest of the Story

Before supplying the financial statements, we declared a dividend and paid to the holding corporation an amount equal to the company's net worth. This left the company insolvent. We then borrowed back enough capital to continue operating and used the assets as collateral to secure the loan.

After reviewing the statements of a corporation that had no equity and whose assets were all attached as security for debt, the attorney for the inventor dropped the suit. The ploy was successful. We won, and I was proud of our victory.

Reader, suppose you are a businessman. Now suppose you are a ruthless and greedy character, but I repeat myself.

Laura Nash

At the time, I rationalized our actions by convincing myself that this is the way business is conducted. I was an engineer, and engineers weren't given ethics courses. We were trained to use the most expedient means to accomplish the task, and morality wasn't generally an issue. I learned my ethics after college from my supervisors and the business community—people whom I looked up to, like Ray. These associations gave me the perception that there was a special set of ethics for business, and it was, in a sense, like football or ice hockey: when you walked out to play, the laws regarding hurting someone changed, and only the game's rules applied on the field.

Several months passed before I began to realize that although this strategy was financially successful, I had demonstrated to the company's employees that I valued profits and performance above doing the right thing. This "victory" cost the company, and me personally, the trust and loyalty of our people. During the following months, our turnover rate went through the roof, and we lost our most valuable people. They just couldn't trust me to look out for their interest when it conflicted with making profits.

Dr. Laura Nash of Harvard University coined the following statement to dramatize the opinion of a large segment of Americans: "Reader, suppose you are a businessman. Now suppose you are a ruthless and a greedy character, but I repeat myself."[1] The perception of these Americans is that the corporate world operates from the

38

position that anything goes as long as you aren't caught and it's good for business. In reality, we have two different issues that are fueling this assumption: companies whose primary goal is to defraud and organizations that are caught in and swept along with the current.

First, there are companies that are created purely as a scam. Their only reason for existing is to defraud people and other companies. Do you remember the New Era Foundation? By soliciting matching funds from an anonymous philanthropist, New Era promised a 100 percent return on the investment of hundreds of nonprofit institutions, including museums, evangelical Christian groups, and hunger relief organizations. In reality, the foundation had no donors, and the charities lost millions of dollars in the fraud. No wonder people don't trust big business.

The second issue is much more prevalent and pervasive. There are many reputable organizations that practice some level of unethical behavior by skirting the law and taking advantage of people and other organizations. These corporations believe that this is the way the game is played, that there is a different set of ethics that apply to business. Their mind-set is that everybody does it, and the system has adjusted itself to accommodate this kind of activity. It's sort of like a company having a bad debt account because they know they are going to have bad debts. This point can be illustrated by a ridiculous but illuminating true story of an "entrepreneur" who steals cars in New Jersey:

> What I do is good for everybody. First of all I create work. I hire men to deliver the cars, . . . maybe drive them out of state, find customers. That's good for the economy, then I'm helping people to get what they could never afford otherwise. A fellow wants a Cadillac but he can't afford it. . . . I save him money. Now he's happy. But so

39

is the guy who lost his car. He gets a nice new Cadillac from the insurance company. The Cadillac company—they're happy too because they sell another Cadillac. The only people who don't do so good is the insurance company, but they're so big that nobody cares personally. They got a budget for this sort of thing anyway. . . . Come on now—who am I really hurting?[2]

In this case, it is easy to see through the thief's argument. But believe me, this perception that taking something from the system isn't really hurting anyone is widespread and is accepted by a significant number of Americans. Few people make the connection between car thefts and insurance premiums, or fudging on their taxes and funding the country. These same citizens work in our commercial establishments and operate our capitalistic machinery. And in the business world, just determining what is right is not always easy, much less mustering the courage to take a stand against something that is advocated by one's coworkers and/or superiors.

It's a Jungle Out There

In the corporate universe, the prime directive is "make a profit," but there are times when one's perception of right and wrong conflicts with this mandate. Take, for example, the following true story. What would you do if you were in this position?

An American computer manufacturing company, with a reputation for having high integrity, sold a multimillion-dollar system to another American corporation for its plant in Mexico. The computer arrived at the destination dock by ship and was promptly unloaded. A standoff ensued when the customs official refused to clear the equipment while he communicated with the

40

computer company's shipping department. When the shipping manager called back, the official told him that five hundred dollars would be required to secure the clearance. The company had a dilemma. It had a strong policy against paying bribes, but the system's components were very sensitive to heat and humidity and could not remain out in the elements for long. The situation reached all the way to the president's desk, and after weighing the options, he decided to pay the Mexican official. He justified his action by saying that this was a normal transaction when doing business in Mexico.[3]

Another situation, which would certainly test one's ethical resolve, was when a group of American business executives were taking a chartered flight out of a Central American country. In the middle of a hot summer day in the tropics, the pilot taxied to the end of the runway of the small airport, cut the engine, turned around, and announced, "I will require two hundred American dollars to take off." Although the company had a policy against paying bribes, the executives paid the pilot. They decided it was the most expedient and probably the safest course of action.

Although these two situations may seem uncommon and are not likely to be experienced by most businesspeople, they are quite common to people who do business internationally. You may not be involved in doing business overseas, but before you decide these kinds of problems don't affect you, let's look at two other examples that involve good people caught in untenable situations.

Between 1979 and 1981, the demand for semiconductors grew so fast that National Semiconductor, a manufacturer of computer semiconductors, felt immense pressure to take shortcuts as the company fell further behind in its attempt to meet contract schedules. The company subsequently admitted that during this period it had gradually omitted the government-required testing and had

41

falsified records to cover the omissions. An employee, testifying before the grand jury, described the situation that
evolved: "When . . . I realized how deeply things were getting falsified, I just couldn't believe it . . . I asked, 'How
did things get the way they were?' Nobody seemed to be
able to give me a good answer."[4] Unfortunately, this man's
comments reflected the bewilderment felt by many of the
employees.

National Semiconductor was fined $1.75 million in
civil and criminal penalties for failing to adequately test
some 26 million semiconductors that were installed in
ships and planes scattered throughout the world and,
unfortunately, could not be traced. I wonder how many
people lost their lives because of these falsifications.

Another sticky situation, one with which I am personally familiar, is that of a California company selling
its wares to a company on the East Coast. At the time,
a friend of mine was in charge of payables for the California firm. Immediately after hiring a new controller,
the East Coast company stopped sending payments for
the products it had purchased. When my friend called
to determine the reason, the controller explained that
in order to get paid, cash equaling one percent must
accompany the invoice, and that the envelope should
be addressed to the controller, marked "confidential."
Of course, the invoice could have been inflated by two
percent to cover the cash and the additional handling
charge. My friend immediately contacted the authori-
ties, and the controller was subsequently fired and
charged with a criminal act.

When reading these stories, it's probably obvious to
you that these situations involve unethical behavior, and
that the individuals involved should have known better.
However, as I said earlier, doing business isn't always that
cut and dried and neither is the advice given to businesspeople. There are authoritative people, well respected,

revered, and considered experts in the field of commerce, who would argue that business should have a special set of ethics. Albert Z. Carr, in an article titled "Is Business Bluffing Ethical?" makes an interesting observation by comparing business and poker:

> No one expects poker to be played on the ethical principles preached in churches. In poker it is right and proper to bluff a friend out of the rewards of being dealt a good hand. A player feels no more than a slight twinge of sympathy, if that, when—with nothing better that a single ace in his hand—he strips a heavy loser, who holds a pair, of the rest of his chips. It was up to the other fellow to protect himself. Poker has a special ethic. . . . No one thinks any worse of poker and no one should think any worse of the game of business because its standards of right and wrong differ from the prevailing traditions of morality in our society.[5]

Dr. Carr's point is that in their office lives businesspeople cease to be private citizens; they become game players who must be guided by a somewhat different ethical standard.

We're Business People, Not Legislators

I admit there are real advantages to being street-smart. Management needs all the edge it can get, and a take-no-prisoners attitude can be an asset in operating a business. It is hard to squeeze out a profit in today's fast-moving international business arena. While you are battling the competition for business and trying to keep the unions at bay, the government keeps legislating more restrictions and regulations. Any edge has to be considered. It is the way the game is played. Carl Kotchian of Lockheed Martin Aeronautics Company justified this position in an illuminating statement:

> If, in a situation where high government officials have influence in matters pertinent to a private company, money is requested as pay-off for those officials, can that private foreign company, which wants its products to be bought at all costs, realistically decline the request on the grounds that it is not ethical?[6]

It's easy to see where he is coming from, isn't it? If Lockheed Martin is going to do business internationally, and that's where the market for aircraft is, they have to compete, and competing may involve paying solicited bribes. If they refuse, they don't get invited to the bidding party; they don't have the opportunity to bid against competing manufacturers from other countries who are faced with the same dilemma or who don't have a problem paying money under the table. Many foreign companies consider bribes a normal expense of doing business. And, after all, there are American jobs at stake and stockholders who expect a return on their investment.

A thing worth having is a thing worth cheating for.

W. C. Fields

William Lawrence said that money and ambition are the major forces that drive our times: "In the time of the greatest economic growth in history, we seem to have sunk to the lowest ethical level in our national experience."[7] As I stated earlier, a significant segment of corporate management believes that a cunning, street-smart management is necessary in order to make a profit in a business environment where fighting the competition and keeping the unions and the government at bay are daily battles. There are those who believe that any edge—making payoffs, giving kickbacks, bribing officials, reducing quality, using deceptive advertising,

44

making unrealistic promises, or other unethical tactics—must be contemplated.

The Nobel Prize–winning economist Milton Friedman advocates this perspective: "There is one and only one social responsibility of business . . . to use its resources to engage in activities designed to increase its profits, so long as it stays within the rules of the game."[8] A survey commissioned by the United States government confirmed this attitude is widespread. It indicated that two-thirds of American corporations *significantly* violate the law.

What to Do?

If the pursuit of profit causes people to act unethically, why not eliminate the motivation? Karl Marx took this position. His philosophy was that "the middle class owner of property must, indeed, be swept out of the way and made impossible."[9] In modern English, he was saying that enterprise ownership should be eliminated and that the profits should be distributed to the workers.

Although Ralph Nader, the consumer advocate, holds a different perspective on societal issues, he believes that businesses do exist to serve the public. Profits should not all be directed to shareholders but should be redistributed in the form of higher wages and benefits to the community:

> The large companies, to be sure, are our major disbursers of income in the form of dividends, interest, and wages. But a concentration of ownership of income misdirects these benefits toward an elite who are already wealthy and away from most Americans who are not.[10]

45

Nader suggested that one solution might be to require that corporations be partially owned by the communities in which they reside. This would insure that some of the dividends would be distributed to these communities and make the organizations more accountable.[11] Certainly he is not suggesting that we adopt a communistic economic structure, but that for-profit organizations, particularly large companies, be responsible for their impact on society. In return for doing business in America, they should contribute more to each community's well-being.

There's a Better Way

Although the experiences related in this chapter might support the premise, "Do unto others *before* they do it unto you," my goal is to demonstrate that profit and ethics go hand in hand. Making a profit and behaving ethically are not mutually exclusive. Companies face many moral dilemmas in conducting business. They are under pressure to do whatever it takes to make a profit and stay afloat. Although many well-respected, nationally known management gurus advocate look-out-for-number-one management, the purpose of this book is to communicate the opposite. Profit is beneficial, indeed necessary, and unethical behavior is not only wrong, but it's bad business and in the long run unprofitable. Although doing what is expedient, even though it's not right, may accomplish the desired result in the short run, such behavior is ultimately self-defeating. People want to work and do business with people they trust and who, they believe, will treat them the way they expect to be treated. In chapter 3 we will argue that profit is a noble and necessary goal of corporate America and good for the average citizen.

Summary

Corporate life isn't easy. With competition breathing down your neck, the government trying to regulate you out of business, and the unions portraying you as just below slumlords, it's hard to maintain your perspective and squeeze out a profit in this light-speed, global business arena. In addition to the real problems faced every day, there is a perception among the American people that corporate boardrooms, like the politician's back rooms, are smoke-filled dens crammed with unsavory characters. Americans relate businesspeople with J. R. Ewing (of the TV program *Dallas*), always scheming to take over some unsuspecting and helpless widow's company while beating out one of his arch rivals in the process.

This perspective has validity. There are some companies that are unscrupulous by design, and there are a significant number of companies that believe they have to compromise their ethics in order to compete in the marketplace. This whole paradigm is fueled by the writings of well-respected business philosophers who contend that the game of business has a special ethic that differs from that of society in general.

My research indicates there is a better way to do business. You don't have to compromise your integrity to be successful in the corporate world. In fact, you will be more successful if you don't play that game. You can have your cake (ethics) and eat it too (be successful)—and sleep peacefully at night.

3

PROFIT IS NOT
A DIRTY WORD

*The trouble with government regulation of
the market is that it prohibits capitalistic acts
between consenting adults.*

Robert Nozick[1]

P rofit shouldn't be a dirty word. Yet most Americans view profit as something unethical, even seamy. People believe that in order for a company to be successful, their success has to come at someone else's expense. It's the perception that the pie is only so big, and for one person to gain a larger piece, someone else must have a smaller one. The following humorous story illustrates this common perception.

A prince was lost in a forest. When at last he reached a clearing he saw a small inn. Being very hungry, he hurried in and ordered a chicken dinner. After he had satisfied his hunger, he asked the proprietor for the bill. The inn-keeper replied, "That will be one hundred dollars." Surprised, the prince said, "I don't understand; there is no shortage of chicken. In fact, I saw quite a few around the inn as I came in." To which the proprietor responded, "There is no shortage of chickens, just a shortage of princes."[2]

This story, which certainly exemplifies the economic axiom of supply and demand, also illustrates the popular perception that America's boardrooms are hotbeds of greedy capitalists where opportunistic companies are ruthlessly maximizing their profits.

The antithesis of this extreme capitalistic philosophy—socialism—aims for economic equality for everyone. Unfortunately, the socialists see making a profit as a constraint to accomplishing this goal. But that's incorrect. To label profit as the major inhibitor of distributing wealth is a little like blaming your car for running out of fuel. Whether you have a socialistic society where everyone shares equally or you have a capitalistic society where entrepreneurship is rewarded, the nation's wealth must be produced, and this requires capital.

Where does this capital come from? R. C. Sproul, president of Ligonier Ministries, has developed a diagram that illustrates the elementary principles involved:

Man's Material Well-being
|
Production
|
Tools
|
Investment Capital
|
Profits

According to Dr. Sproul, "Man's physical life is dependent upon production." Someone must produce the material goods required for people's well-being. If we are going to provide food, clothing, and shelter for ourselves, not to mention big screen TVs with surround sound, we must produce the goods necessary to meet these needs. Certainly, tools are among the most important elements needed for production. As Dr. Sproul points out, "The reason a peasant in a backward country cannot produce as much food as a farmer in the industrialized West is that . . . the western farmer has at his disposal labor-saving devices which increase production."[3]

Next-generation tools are developed and produced through research, using profits as the funding mechanism. Without profit there would be no new tools developed or built because there would be no resources available or incentive to build them. Profit provides the resources needed for the development and manufacture of new tools that increase production.

Another requirement for production is investment capital. Companies can't operate without capital. The Western farmer can go to a bank and borrow the capital needed to purchase a technologically advanced piece of equipment, provided he or she is credit worthy, but the loan must be paid back. Ultimately, profit, presumably created by using the new equipment, provides the means of repayment. Capital is the fuel that makes the industrial engine run, and capital cannot be attracted without the provider getting something in return.

Profit Ain't a Four-Letter Word

The "something in return" is profit. If society wants Aunt Tilly to invest her hard-earned retirement dollars in the stock market, providing the capital for companies to expand and produce more basic goods and more big screen TVs with surround sound, she will need a reasonable return on her investment. Otherwise, she would be better off putting her money in a tin can and hiding it under her mattress. No one would knowingly invest in a corporation that isn't making a profit because it won't be around long.

America is the most entrepreneurial country that has ever existed. Why? Because our capitalistic society fosters individual and corporate creativity and encourages entrepreneurial activity, which by its very nature involves both risk and rewards. In founding Pioneer Manufacturing Inc. (PMI), which I still own, my wife and I worked for over three years, putting in over two thousand hours evenings and weekends, before we received a dollar out of it. Why would we do this knowing that it might fail and we might lose everything? We did it because of the hope that a successful return on the investment of time and money would justify the risk.

Every time a new company is founded or an existing company produces a product or service without payment in advance, it is taking a risk. The new company could fail, or the existing company might not sell its product or service. Profit is often directly related to risk. As a friend of mine, Mark Gill, president of Rogers Capital Group, says, "Profit is the reward for taking the risk."

We all need motivation, and money is the universal motivator—not because we are a society of greedy people but because money is a resource that provides food, shelter, clothing, options, and a measure of freedom. As I write this, PMI has just completed its best year in terms of sales and profits. Ten months into our fiscal year, our profits were strong, but our sales were not as good as we would have liked. With two months left in the fiscal calendar, our president, Randy Kozak, proposed an experiment. He announced he would give a bonus of one thousand dollars to each employee at PMI if we could sell, produce, and ship enough product to finish the year with 10 percent more sales than last year. In order to succeed, the last two months would both have to be record months. He knew that if we made it, we would also produce record profits.

I was skeptical, to say the least, because as an industrial engineer, I had a good understanding of our production capabilities and limitations. From a practical standpoint, we just didn't have the capacity to do it, and I gave the program little chance of success. When I told Randy this, he said, "I don't know how it can be done, but if the motivation is there, I believe we'll make it."

"Well," I said, "what if you miss it by only a small amount?"

He responded, "If we miss it by ten dollars, we don't get the bonus. That's the risk we take."

Well, you guessed it. We made it, and not only did we hit our goal, we exceeded it. Instead of 10 percent, we were 12 percent over last year.

When I reflect on the program, it amazes me that our people could sell and produce that much volume with the limited manpower, equipment, and resources that were available. I still don't understand the dynamics; however, I do know it started with the bonus. Then it took on a life of its own, with its own motivation. Our capitalistic society provides for this kind of achievement. Of all the economic systems man has devised, capitalism provides the best incentive to succeed.

Oh, What a Convoluted Web We Weave

You may remember the great UPS strike of August 1997. Although it only lasted a few weeks, it had a devastating impact on shipping in America, particularly on companies that rely on inexpensive transport of their packages. UPS is big; its 2,400 facilities employ 147,000 delivery trucks and 218 aircraft to ship an average of 12 million packages worldwide every day. UPS had 80 percent of the small package market, and when its workers went on strike, the effect was devastating. With four-fifths of the U.S. shipping capacity shut down, the shippers had no place to turn. The strike crippled the whole country.

The Teamsters Union called the strike because, according to Ron Carey, the Teamsters' president, the UPS work force was 57 percent part-time workers. These part-time employees deserved but didn't enjoy the same benefits as the full-time people.

UPS officials contended they needed to keep this basic operating structure to keep costs in line. These employees were only needed for four or five hours a day during peak shipping operations. UPS made just over $1 billion in profits in 1996. Big bucks? Not really, just 4.4 percent of revenues. They contended that under the union's plan, by the third year of the contract, the settlement would cost over $1 billion. Obviously, these costs would have to be made up somewhere else or passed on to the customer. The company couldn't operate at a loss because the stockholders expect a return on their investment. Basic business stuff, right? Well, read on.

Each party's position, as reported by the *Wall Street Journal*, is shown on the chart on the following page.

Actually, the issues surrounding the strike were more basic. The real issue was *control of the pension fund*. The UPS management wanted to withdraw from the multi-employer pension controlled solely by the Teamsters and create an independent plan for its workers. Of course, this would be a financial disaster for the

54

Teamsters and UPS Proposals

	Teamsters' position	UPS's position
Contract	Five or more years.	Two to three years.
Jobs	Convert 3,000 or more part-time jobs to full-time per year.	Convert 1,000 part-time jobs to full-time per year.
Wages & Salary Increases	Specific increases were not disclosed.	$1.50 to $2.50 per hour over five years.
Pensions & Benefits	Retain the current pension plan.	Withdraw from the multi-employer plan and create a UPS plan.

union because they would no longer have total control of, and use of, one of the largest sources of pension money in America.

The final agreement, as usual, was a compromise:

- Five-year contract
- Convert 10,000 or more part-time jobs to full-time over five years
- Part-time jobs increase $4.10 per hour and full-time jobs increase $3.30 per hour over five years
- Retain the current pension plan

The union got what it wanted most: *to keep control of the pension fund.* Interestingly, it would take almost two years for the employees to recoup the cost of striking from the additional money generated by the raises.

The perplexing twist to all of this is that *UPS was an employee-owned company, and this ownership includes part-time people.* In essence, the employees were striking against themselves.[4] This is a little like me, the owner of my company, striking for a higher salary! It seems to me that the employees walked out on themselves, and the strike cost them a lot of money, both as employees and as owners.

55

A much more effective way for the employees to express their grievances would have been to approach the board (all of whom came up through the ranks from entry-level jobs) as stockholders. As owners, they could have simply ordered management to comply.

This story, as convoluted as it is, highlights the deeply rooted misconception about profit and ownership among the rank and file in America. The UPS employees didn't see themselves as owners living the American dream, but as loyal union members fighting for their rights and the rights of others. They had difficulty comprehending that the huge profit is actually a small percentage of revenues and that their actions directly affected the value of each employee's investment.

The Invisible Hand

In his famous discourse, *The Wealth of Nations*, Adam Smith postulated the "invisible hand" theory. His premise was that as an individual endeavors to produce goods and services to provide income, he or she is contributing to the commerce of society in general. Even though this individual does not intend to promote the public good, promoting his own interest directs effort to the greater benefit of society, as if led by an "invisible hand." As Smith noted, "In fact, I have never known much good done by those who affected [whose intention was] to trade for the public good."[5] Smith would agree that every person should enjoy the fruits of his labor. Then, and only then, do these fruits provide an incentive to create new enterprises or to expand existing ones, thereby improving everyone's standard of living.

Peter Drucker, the revered management philosopher, appears to agree with Smith. In his classic book *Manage-*

ment, Dr. Drucker writes that the primary emphasis of a business enterprise should be economic performance:

> While by no means the only task [of a business enterprise] to be discharged in society, it [economic performance] is the primary task, because all other social tasks—education, health care, defense, and the advancement of knowledge—depend on the surplus of economic resources, i.e., profits and other savings, which only successful economic performance can produce. The more of these other satisfactions we want, and the more highly we value them, the more we depend on economic performance of business enterprise.[6]

In the same section, he emphasizes that business managers must always put economic performance first when planning and making decisions.

A fortuitous endorsement of profit is also found in the New Testament. I include this passage because Christ never owned anything and making a profit in the traditional sense certainly wasn't a priority, but this parable endorses the importance of profitable financial management:

> A man going into another country . . . called together his servants and loaned them money to invest while he was gone. He gave $5,000 to one, $2,000 to another, and $1,000 to the last—dividing it in the proportion of their ability—then left on his trip. The man who received the $5,000 began immediately to buy and sell with it and soon earned another $5,000. The man with the $2,000 went right to work, too, and earned another $2,000. But the man who received the $1,000 dug a hole in the ground and hid the money for safekeeping. After a long time their master returned from his trip and called them to him to account for his money. The man to whom he had entrusted the $5,000 brought him $10,000. His mas-

ter praised him for good work. "You have been faithful in handling this small amount," he told him, "so now I will give you many more responsibilities." . . . Next came the man who had received $2,000, with the report, "Sir, you gave me $2,000 to use, and I doubled it." "Good work," his master said. "You are a good and faithful servant. You have been faithful over this small amount so now I will give you much more." Then the man with the $1,000 came and said, "Sir, I knew you were a hard man . . . so I hid your money in the earth and here it is." But his master replied, "Wicked man! Lazy slave . . . you should at least have put my money in the bank where it would draw interest."[7]

The master fired the servant because he didn't earn a profit. Although Christ was illustrating another point, he was also endorsing a return on capital, and so am I. An interesting note—the interest charged at that time was 12 percent per year.

Profit = Blessings – Clothes

Most of us think of profit in monetary terms, usually as a percentage of revenues. John Stieber tells a story that gives insight into the need for profit over the long haul on a personal level:

There was once an immigrant tailor who came to this country and opened up a shop. One day, his son, who was an accountant, dropped by for a visit. While he was there, he noticed two cigar boxes sitting next to the cash register. One was labeled "paid bills" and the other was labeled "unpaid bills." The son chastised the father for keeping his records in such a manner because the old tailor didn't know what his profit was. The father lovingly put his arm around his son's shoulders and told

58

him that when he came to this country, many years ago, the only things he owned were his clothes. Now he has a home, a car, a good business, good health, a daughter who is a college professor, a daughter who is a nuclear engineer, and a son who is not too sharp an accountant. The old tailor then said, "When I add up all of my blessings and subtract the clothes on my back, what remains is my profit."[8]

Most of us would agree that the profit the old tailor made over the years was ethical, even honorable, and we certainly don't begrudge him these blessings. Well, most American businesses are small and are run by honest, hardworking people who have a similar story. Making a profit to them means being able to replace the ten-year-old car, buy clothes for their family, and pay for their children's college tuition.

Summary

Contrary to popular opinion, making a profit doesn't necessarily mean creating pollution, operating unsafe factories, exploiting people, or wasting natural resources. To earn a return on an investment of people, materials, and capital over the long haul requires wise conservation of these resources. A wise manager will protect, preserve, and nurture them, much as a farmer will care for the land that yields his harvest.

If America is going to provide food, clothing, and shelter for its population, commerce must be able to produce the goods to meet these needs, and the for-profit corporation is one of the most efficient institutions ever devised to accomplish this. Profit is a necessary ingredient for powering the economic machinery. Without profit, there would be no capital to replace aging tech-

59

nology, to expand and increase production, to increase the living standard of the nation, or to generate surplus goods to feed the hungry of the world. It really doesn't matter if you are philosophically a socialist or an entrepreneur; our economic power plant has to generate more power than it consumes.

Profit shouldn't be a dirty word. None of us would criticize the old tailor for creating the resources needed to buy a home, replace his aging car, or put his children through college. When viewed in this context, profit is a very positive thing.

PART 2

ETHICS AND SUCCESS:
TWO SIDES OF THE SAME COIN

In general, the morals of all societies are

similar. Although they disagree over some

points, behavior such as selfishness and

deceitfulness are universally unacceptable.

C. S. Lewis

4

BEING ETHICAL ISN'T PROFITABLE
. . . OR IS IT?

We're not in the business of making
automobiles; we're in the business of making
money.

Anonymous[1]

In chapter 3, we made a case for profit being a necessary ingredient in our society. Now I want to focus
on ethics as a way of promoting long-term profits
and stability within the organization.

"Two days before we were to submit our bid on a government contract in which the low bid wins, a brown
paper bag showed up with our competitor's bid in it,"
recalled Norman Augustine, chairman of Lockheed
Martin Corporation. "We didn't spend ten minutes delib-
erating over the appropriate action to take." Augustine

contacted the government agency involved, turned the information over to them, and contacted the competitor. Then Lockheed Martin submitted their bid unchanged and lost the contract. "As a result, some of our employees lost their jobs and our shareholders lost money."[2]

It's really not that difficult to see the ethical dilemma in this case: either be ethical or lose money. However, Augustine believes that although doing the right thing cost Lockheed Martin in the short run, "We established a reputation that in the long run will draw us business, and it's naive to equate good ethics with profits in the short run."[3]

Although the decision in this case was painful, it was clear-cut ethically. However, another situation Augustine faced was more complex. As a contractor launching spacecraft for the air force, Lockheed Martin receives a substantial bonus when a vehicle is launched successfully. "One day our insurance department heard about an insurance policy that would insure our launch bonus for a low premium," said Augustine. "For one nickel on the dollar we could guarantee the dollar." It was a win win for Lockheed Martin. If the launch were successful, it would get the bonus; if the launch were unsuccessful, the insurance company would pay the bonus.

The ethical dilemma facing the company: Were they negating the purpose of the bonus? The customer, the U.S. government, was paying the bonus to ensure that Lockheed Martin would do everything in its power to make the launch successful. Taking the insurance policy might undermine that purpose. Augustine consulted the company's engineers to see if the bonus insurance would make a difference in their attitude or performance. The engineers declared that "they would do everything in their power to make the launch successful in any case," and he believed them. They were dedicated professionals. The company's outside counsel agreed and advised that Lockheed Martin had a fiduciary responsibility to take the insurance.

Augustine still didn't feel right about it, so he called his customer, a NASA official, to get the space agency's reaction, to see if they cared one way or the other. After considering the matter for several days, the official called back and reported that they cared a lot. "We finally decided not to buy the insurance," noted Augustine, "and yes, we eventually had a loss."[4]

This account of corporate ethics gives me a warm feeling, not only in my heart but also in my wallet. Our *taxes* pay the bonus!

You Can't Be Highly Ethical *and* Make Money, Can You?

Can a company be too ethical? There are those who believe it can. In the article "Can a Company Be Too Ethical?" Wharton School's Edward Bowman writes, "Can a company concerned with its overall health spend too much money on social responsibility? . . . The answer is yes . . . you can spend too much time, too much effort, on almost anything."

In the same article, Andrew Singer gives convincing reasons for limiting the amount of time and effort on social ethics:

> What happens to a company in a highly competitive industry where sharp practices are the norm? If it behaves too nobly, might not other corporations succeed in cutting it off at the knees? Or what about companies that pour out heaps of money into safety or environmental compliance—above and beyond want is mandated by law? Won't that hurt the bottom line?

65

Dr. Singer goes on to say, "A company, too, can pay so much attention to 'doing good' that its traditional business suffers."[5] There is no question that he makes a good point.

John Delaney, professor of management at the University of Iowa, has done research that indicates that some corporate executives believe a company can be too ethical. He cites an example of a pharmaceutical company that curtailed its internal auditing function because it became too aggressive in investigating its drug testing documentation. The conclusion was that the audit not only cost money but it could also uncover data that indicated failing results.[6]

Dr. Bowman's study examined one hundred companies in the food processing industry to establish the relationship between corporate social responsibility and profits. The study found that as social responsibility increased so did profit—to a point. After that point, the relationship diminished.[7]

Thomas Shanks, executive director of the Markkula Center for Applied Ethics, relates a case based on a true story of a stock and bond brokerage firm owning 20 percent of a particular mutual fund. To promote the fund, the brokerage house offered its salespeople an incentive. For $500,000 in sales of this fund the salesperson would receive double credits and a five-day "due diligence" trip to a European or U.S. resort.

Although the firm had a policy against sales contests on mutual funds, it circumvented the policy by claiming this was not a sales contest, and the trip was "informational" and related to due diligence. Also, the firm said, "No pressure is applied . . . to sell a particular product." The firm considered the trips "advanced training."[8]

Was the promotion successful? Of course, it was a good business decision. The salespeople, when they had a choice, would push this fund. Was the practice unethical? I certainly think it was. The customers, most of them unsophisticated investors and not trained in stock and bond research, were relying on the salesperson's expertise to find the best investment.

Most executives charged with making profits, the corporate decision makers, *disagree* with the view that a company can be too ethical. When Tom Stevens, chairman and CEO of the Mansville Corporation, was asked why he added warning labels to fiberglass products going to Japan even though such precautions were not required, indeed not even recommended by the Japanese government, he replied, "A human being in Japan is no different from a human being in the U.S."[9] This action cost Mansville 40 percent of its business in Japan, but the loss was short-lived. Ultimately, Mansville was able to recoup its Japanese business.

For other endorsements of ethical business behavior, look at the published writings of corporate executives such as Max DePree of Herman Miller Inc., LaRue Tone Hosmer of Hosmer Machine Company (who also has a Ph.D. from Harvard University), and Jack Faris, president of NFIB. Also read the works of those close to industry, such as Tom Peters, Peter Drucker, and Stephen Covey. For these advocates of corporate ethics, there is no economic constraint or limit on doing the right thing.

Lockheed Martin's Augustine says it well: "So called bad outcomes are only in the short run. It always pays off in the long run. To me, the subject of ethics deals with principles—what you believe to be right or wrong— it's impossible to be too ethical. You can't have too many principles."[10]

Augustine's position is confirmed by a survey done by Dr. Laura Nash. Thousands of middle- and top-level executives were asked about their personal values and business practices, and she discovered that the same set of values, with little variation, drives most managers both at home and at work. These values are:

Honesty	Family
Integrity	Achievement
Trustworthiness	Reliability
Respect for other people	Fairness
Self-respect	Loyalty

Love, religion, and hard work were also often cited.[11] Why would managers employ these values in their business practices if they were detrimental to their careers? The answer is simple: they wouldn't. These values are learned and passed down from the older managers to the younger ones because they are good business, both for the individual and the organization.

Is Being Ethical Really Profitable?

Research indicates that those who believe there is a limit to the value of ethics—not social programs, but doing right—are misinformed. Much evidence demonstrates that good ethics is good business because of simple quid pro quo concepts: A business that behaves ethically induces others to behave ethically toward it. In the *Harvard Business Review* article "Personal Values and Business Decisions," episodes drawn from many different sectors of the business community support this position. For example:

- A firm exercises particular care in meeting all responsibilities to its employees. As a result, it is rewarded with an unusual degree of employee loyalty, application, and productivity.

- A supplier refuses to exploit the advantage of a seller's market and retains the loyalty and continued business of customers when conditions change to a buyer's market.
- A firm employs persons with disabilities and discovers they are often more productive, hardworking, and loyal than other employees.

The article also supports the view that good ethics is good business by stressing the dangers and probable penalties inherent in unethical business behavior:

- A customer is dealt with unfairly and thereafter refuses to deal with the supplier in question. Other firms, learning of the situation, also refuse to deal with the supplier because it has shown it can't be trusted.
- A firm allows its salespeople to disseminate misleading information about its competitors' products. This invites open retaliation by competing salespeople who reveal the truth. [12]

To sum up the argument of this article: People want to do business with people they trust, and they don't want to do business with people they don't trust.

One company that subscribes to the theory that doing right is good business is the ServiceMaster Corporation, the $3 billion sales company of Chicago, Illinois. It prides itself on adhering to ethical principles. Included in the company's mission statement is the following: "To grow profitably, to pursue excellence, to help people develop, to honor God in all that we do." According to Chairman C. William Pollard, making sure the company honors God in all that it does is the best management principle ever devised. It sets a clear direction, eliminates ethical dilemmas, and makes distinguishing between right and wrong easy, all of which make management easy.

This book isn't about honoring God (although being a Christian, I believe ethical principles are from God); it is about being ethical and making a profit. And this approach seems to work. ServiceMaster recorded increased revenues and profits for twenty-three straight years, with revenues growing at a compounded annual rate of 19 percent per year and profits at 22 percent annually over the same period.[13]

The Empirical Research

You may be tempted to skip over this next section, but it's very important that you understand where I stand and why. The premise of this book is that there is a valid connection between ethics and profits.

For his doctoral dissertation at Georgia State University, Walter Thomas Jr. conducted a study of the relationships among business ethics, religion, and organizational performance. The research found a significant positive correlation between a firm's ethical measure and its economic performance. Also, he found an inverse relationship existed between its ethics and the employee turnover. The higher the company's ethics, the less turnover the company experienced. Losing employees and retraining new ones is a significant expense that is seldom mentioned in relation to ethics because it reflects on management's performance.[14]

A recent survey by the Center for Economic Revitalization, a Vermont-based investment research group, found that companies with strong support for public service programs and responsible employee relations grew much faster over the past decade than did other

70

companies. During the study period, the Dow Jones average rose 55 percent, whereas companies identified as having strong ethical and value-related philosophies increased 240 percent.

An ethical attitude toward environmental issues has also shown to be beneficial to corporate growth. In a study conducted by Bragdon and Marlin of the Council on Economic Priorities, five different measures of financial performance were used to determine that the companies within the paper and pulp industry that had the best record on pollution control and the environment were also the most profitable.[15]

James Burke, chairman of Johnson and Johnson Pharmaceuticals, reported to the Advertising Council that he had "found evidence that suggests that those companies that organize their businesses around the broad concept of public service over the long run, provide superior performance for their stockholders." A Johnson and Johnson team compiled a list of twenty-six companies that were driven by a simple moral principle: serving the public (in the broadest sense, not necessarily their customers) better than their competition. The study showed an 11 percent growth per annum in profits compounded over thirty years. The rise was three times the growth of the gross national product, which grew at just over 3 percent during the same period.[16]

In a similar study, Franklin Research and Development found that the stocks in those companies included in *The Best 100 Companies to Work for in America* dramatically outperformed the Standard & Poors 500 stock price average over a ten-year period. The "Best 100 Companies" stocks rose from a value of just over one hundred in 1975 to seven hundred in 1985, whereas the Standard & Poors 500 rose from the same amount to only slightly above the two hundred level.[17]

Touche Ross, the accounting firm, surveyed 1,082 corporate directors and officers, business school deans, and members of Congress for their views on ethics in American business. The study found that 63 percent of respondents believed that companies improve their competitive position by maintaining high ethical standards. Only a minority, 14 percent, felt that companies with high ethics were weaker competitors, and 23 percent said ethics had no effect on their competitive position.[18]

One of the most comprehensive studies from a longevity standpoint comes from Dr. Louis H. Grossman of the Lincoln Center for Applied Ethics, a department of Arizona State University. He studied eight New York Exchange firms that paid dividends consecutively for *one hundred years*. He wanted to know how and why these companies were so successful.

Dr. Grossman identified six characteristics that these firms embodied throughout this period. Five of these dealt with the companies' business savvy and long-term strategies, but one characteristic is germane to this discussion. Dr. Grossman determined that for a company to be successful over the long haul, it must have a strong ethical value system and communicate those values to its employees. He said, "Priorities determined policies. Over time everyone on the payroll acted upon priorities enunciated about people, profits, products, and productivity."[19]

Numerous other empirical studies confirm that being ethical is profitable. A study conducted by M. Zetlin revealed that fifteen Fortune 500 companies that employed written ethical principles for over twenty years grew twice as fast as the average Fortune 500 company.[20] A study by S. M. Rao and J. B. Hamilton found that publicized *unethical* conduct has a negative effect on the shareholders of a company by lowering the price of the stock.[21]

My Research

When conducting a qualitative research project, the investigation must be carried out in accordance with strict requirements. This means it has to comply with scientific research criteria and be statistically valid. This is good; however, the findings also have to be devoid of opinion, embellishment, and humor, which doesn't make for good reading. As I said about the previous research, this evidence is included to demonstrate that the benefits of being ethical can be empirically studied and to help people understand my position. The good news is that I'm going to lighten it up a bit, summarize the study, and discuss only the highlights.

My research investigated the interaction between ethical conduct and economic performance of publicly held companies from all industries. We compared the company's ethics with their profitability to see if they correlated. Ethics were defined by identifying the majority of ethical dilemmas faced by the corporate community and condensing them into the moral principles underlying the situations. We then condensed them into four moral principles that covered the majority of ethical situations faced by businesspeople.

1. **Don't deceive.** Don't misrepresent, withhold information, or give misleading information. Joseph Levine jokingly said, "You can fool all the people all of the time if the advertising is right and the budget is big enough." He's probably right, to a point, but in the long run, deception costs you in trust and reputation.
2. **Don't covet.** Coveting includes being selfish and having an unreasonable desire for something that

73

doesn't belong to you. The grass isn't greener on the other side; it's greener where you water it.

3. **Don't steal.** A lady sent a check to the IRS for $300 with a note saying, "I cheated on my income tax and haven't been able to sleep since. This check covers half of what I owe. If I continue having trouble sleeping, I'll send the other half." Although we can all sympathize with her, there are better ways to deal with the IRS.

4. **Do unto others as you would have them do unto you.** J. C. Penney built his retailing organization on this principle: "Treat our customers and our employees like we want to be treated."

We then created twenty-four vignettes involving ethical situations to reflect these moral dilemmas. Here is one of the vignettes.

A company is considering purchasing three identical and adjoining parcels of land to create a plant site. Two of the properties are owned by investors and will cost $110,000 each. A farmer who is asking $50,000 owns the third. Even though there is no difference in the three parcels, the company's manager decides, since the prices are confidential, to pay the farmer only what he is asking. Was the manager's position ethical?

A verification committee of twenty-two business-people and professionals, all with credentials qualifying them to judge whether behavior was ethical or unethical, conducted a pretest before the vignette survey was offered to the corporate subjects. The vignettes were scored on a scale from one to five to determine if the action taken was ethical or unethical. As you might guess, the committee scored the action in the above situation as unethical. However, the majority of companies responding to the research said to give the farmer what he was asking.

Using the data collected from the vignette survey, as well as published financial information of the publicly held companies, we were able to correlate their ethics with their financial performance. Although we were not able to reject the null hypothesis, using multiple regression we confirmed the findings of the studies mentioned earlier in this chapter: Being ethical is profitable.

An interesting bit of information serendipitously emerged from the study. Managers become more ethical as they age. The most significant discovery was a strong correlation between aging and the Golden Rule: Do unto others as you would have them do unto you. Why do you think this correlation was so strong? I believe it's simply because older managers have more experience with the consequences of good and bad judgment. This would confirm Dr. Nash's "Personal Values and Business Practices" survey discussed earlier.

Summary

Just as there are laws of nature governing the physical world, there are also principles that influence both the business world as well as our private lives. Like Adam Smith's "invisible hand," these influences cause those who do right to be more successful. These are natural laws (we Christians believe they are God's laws given for man's benefit), and they work. They work regardless of the motives of the people involved.

Certainly, unethical behavior can accomplish its purpose in the short run; we saw that in the second chapter. However, as in the laws of probability, whether a coin flipped one time will land on heads or tails cannot be predicted, but if it is flipped one million times, the outcome can be predicted with a high degree of certainty. Gambling houses are built (and are able to attract financing) on the principle that over a statistically valid number of events, the odds will always produce a profit for the house. So it is with the laws of ethics. A business can be successful by operating unethically for a short time. Unethical behavior will not be successful in the long run, however, because it violates laws of human nature. The empirical studies cited give overwhelming evidence that this is true. Also, it's intuitive. People like doing business with, working for, or just having a relationship with people they trust.

5

THE WHITE KNIGHT CARRIED
A BLUE SHIELD

We're all in the business of making money,
but you have to be able to look at yourself in
the mirror each morning.

Kathy Birk, Dean Witter

Jack, a friend and former coworker, cares a great deal for people. For twelve years he was our vice president of operations at Pioneer, and during that time, he spent an inordinate amount of time and energy agonizing over his employees' personal problems.

Several years ago, Jack hired a young man not because the youth was the most qualified for the position but because he needed work. Although Jack was normally very responsible in his hiring practices and selected only the most qualified candidates, this time his compassion outweighed his good judgment. Ron only lasted a few months. The time finally came when Jack could no longer tolerate his irresponsible behavior.

Under the COBRA insurance law, a discharged employee has the option of continuing the company's group insurance for eighteen months after termination. It's designed to allow time for a person to get reestablished with another company or to acquire insurance elsewhere. Ron declined the coverage but failed to sign the waiver.

Three weeks after leaving Pioneer, Ron was riding a motorcycle in a fifty-five mph speed zone when an elderly lady driving a full-size car pulled out in front of him. He hit her broadside. The force catapulted him over the car and headfirst into the concrete pavement.

Suffering multiple head injuries and spinal cord damage, Ron lay comatose for three days. The doctors said if he lived, he would be a quadriplegic for the rest of his life. He would never be able to care for himself and would require constant care and attention.

As time passed, Ron's condition gradually improved to the point where his doctors felt confident he would live. However, short of a miracle, he would always be paralyzed from the neck down.

The community where Pioneer is located is small, rural, and close-knit. Ron's grandmother owned the local restaurant where the townspeople gathered. The whole town knew about his accident and was anxious for Ron. Jack had been monitoring the situation every day and was deeply concerned for Ron and his family, as were the rest of us at Pioneer.

The Cobra Strikes

One Monday afternoon, our controller, Vicki Hilliard, called Jack and me into her office and told us that Ron hadn't signed the insurance waiver and was still eligible for our insurance under the COBRA law. Jack and I looked at each other as she continued, "We have an ethical dilemma: whether to tell his family that he still has the right to pick up the insurance even though he verbally declined it when he left Pioneer." And then she gave us the bad news: "I have done some checking. If he does pick up the insurance, with his medical bills soaring, our insurance company will surely raise our rates to cover the additional expense. This could get *very* expensive."

As difficult as the decision was, we really had no choice. We went to the family and told them he was still eligible for our medical insurance if they wanted to continue the coverage. Of course, since he had no other insurance, they elected to take advantage of the COBRA provision and reinstated the policy.

As expected, Ron's medical bills had already exceeded hundreds of thousands of dollars and were headed into the millions. As a twenty-two-year-old quadriplegic, the cost of his daily care and maintenance for the rest of his life was going to be astronomical. For Pioneer, we knew this would translate into significant insurance premium increases, but we had no idea how much.

A few weeks later, just before the annual insurance renewal date, our insurance company notified us our premiums would increase *over 300 percent,* from $290 per employee per month to over $800. There was no way we could absorb that kind of cost increase. At that point, we had a year left on Ron's COBRA coverage. The increase would mean that we would operate at a significant loss for more than a year.

We began contacting other insurance carriers even though we knew they would have to assume Ron's medical expenses, which meant that there was little to no chance that another company would cover us. We were right. None of the carriers we talked to would take on a client knowing they were going to lose money.

We reviewed our options. The first choice was to pay the high premiums for the period left on the COBRA plan. This option would cause us to lose a significant amount of money at a time when we didn't have the resources to absorb the losses. We would have to borrow money to continue operating and to cover the losses created by the additional premiums. A second option was to drop our health insurance, give the employees a raise equal to the existing premiums, and let each employee find their own insurance. This option was particularly distasteful because some of our employees were not insurable as individuals because of preexisting conditions, a common situation in many companies. They would have to go without insurance during this period.

The 5 Percent Decision

This situation reminds me of a speech given by Willard Butcher, past chairman of Chase Manhattan Corporation, to a college graduating class. "You're going to find that 95 percent of all the decisions you'll ever make in your business career could be made as well by a reasonably intelligent high school sophomore," he told the students. "But they'll pay you for the other 5 percent." It's this 5 percent that will cause sleepless nights and require periods of deep contemplation, long walks to sort things out, and serious discussions with people whose opinion you value and trust. Our insurance quandary was one of those 5 percent decisions, and because Pioneer's management team is made up of Christians, it also required periods of deep prayer.

After much prayer, soul searching, and revisiting of our core principles, we decided on the first option. We would keep the insurance, pay the higher premiums, and try to absorb the losses. Our people deserved our loyalty.

I Never Thought the White Knight Would Be an Insurance Company!

Blue Cross and Blue Shield of Tennessee had been monitoring our situation and counseling us throughout this painful insurance dilemma. We had used them as a resource for information regarding the health insurance environment and about our rights and options. Within a week of our decision, the representative contacted our controller and said, "Our evaluation committee and I have discussed your situation at length. They are impressed with the way you conducted yourselves during this crisis, the decision you made, and the loyalty you displayed toward your employees." She also said, "As a health insurance provider, we believe we should accept some responsibility toward the community we serve." Then she gave us the good news: "If we can limit our exposure and spread the cost of the next year over several years, we will take Pioneer as a client." She went on to explain that they believed that over the long haul a relationship with us would be profitable if we would commit to keeping the insurance with Blue Cross for three years, provided they didn't significantly increase the premium or change the benefits.

The rate Blue Cross offered was $440 per employee. Although this was $150 above the original cost, it was significantly less than the cost of our existing policy and would allow Pioneer to operate at about a break-even point. We were so taken aback that we actually challenged her. Was she sure that Blue Cross knew what they were committing to? She assured us that they had stud-

81

ied it at length and understood the risk, adding, "This is what we have reserves for, and we feel good about the decision."

That year we did indeed break even. We even made a little money. But the best part was that we were able to provide health insurance to all of our employees and meet our obligations without borrowing money. Blue Cross lost money on us that year, but in the following years, we were able to operate at a good claims ratio, which allowed them to make up the losses, and the relationship became profitable.

Summary

How does this story relate to ethics and profits? According to Blue Cross, had we decided to drop the existing insurance, causing our employees to find their own insurance, they wouldn't have taken us as a client. Because we approached the problem from an ethical perspective and put our employees' well-being above short-term profit, they felt we would be a good risk in the long run. This gave them confidence that we would do all we could to provide our people with a safe work environment and not expose them to health hazards. Our decision also assured them that we would conduct business with Blue Cross and Blue Shield in an ethical manner.

One of the intangible benefits of committing to provide insurance for our employees during this period was the loyalty it fostered. This allegiance translated into lower turnover and greater productivity. This, of course, lowered the cost of hiring and training and improved quality. Yes, doing the right thing can promote profits as evidenced by this real-life situation that the Pioneer employees and I lived through.

6

The Good, the Bad, and the Ugly

I don't like blood; I'm a businessman, blood is a big expense.

The Godfather

Okay, we've seen examples of how ethical business practices can be profitable. Now let's discuss how unethical business practices can be unprofitable. According to an article written by Frank Navran in March 1998, *ABC News* reported that lying, cheating, and stealing cost the average organization $700 per employee per year. Navran also said that Navran Associates' (his consulting firm) experiences with various clients suggest that the single most important intangible cost might be displaced employee commitment and creativity. Employees who feel they have been mistreated by their employers "resort to . . . silent sabotage. They use their creativity and intelligence to punish the organization or beat the systems." Conversely, "When that creativity is redirected toward helping the organization reach its goals and making the systems work better, overall organization performance improves from 10 percent to 20 percent." According to Navran, "Bottom line—We conservatively estimate the value of reducing ethical conflict at between $3000 and $5000 per employee per year."[1]

Dr. Laura Nash, the Harvard University professor mentioned earlier, compiled a list of thirty unethical acts from a survey of business executives with whom she has worked. This list, although not exhaustive, is representative of unethical behavior found in the workplace.

1. Greed
2. Cover-ups and misrepresentations in reporting and control procedures
3. Misleading product or service claims
4. Reneging or cheating on negotiated terms
5. Establishing policies that are likely to cause others to lie to get the job done
6. Overconfidence in one's own judgment to the risk of the corporate entity
7. Disloyalty to the company as soon as times get rough
8. Poor quality
9. Humiliating people at work or by stereotypes in advertising
10. Lockstep obedience to authority, however unethical and unfair it may be
11. Self-aggrandizement over corporate obligations (conflict of interest)
12. Favoritism

13. Price fixing
14. Sacrificing the innocent and helpless in order to get things done
15. Suppression of basic rights: freedom of speech, choice, and personal relationships
16. Failing to speak up when unethical practices occur
17. Neglect of one's family or of one's personal needs
18. Making a product decision that perpetrates a questionable safety issue
19. Not putting back what you take out of the environment, employees, and/or corporate assets
20. Knowingly exaggerating the advantages of a plan in order to get needed support
21. Failing to address areas of bigotry, sexism, or racism
22. Courting the business hierarchy versus doing the job well
23. Climbing the corporate ladder by stepping on others
24. Promoting the destructive go-getter who outruns his mistakes
25. Failing to cooperate with other areas of the company—the enemy mentality
26. Lying by omission to employees for the sake of the business
27. Making an alliance with a questionable partner, albeit for a good cause
28. Not taking responsibility for injurious practices—intentional or not
29. Abusing or just going along with corporate perks that waste money and time
30. Corrupting the public political process through legal means[2]

In chapter 9, we will group these acts by the ethical precept they violate and discuss the underlying principles. But first it's important that we look at the problems created by these acts and see how unethical behavior ultimately reduces income.

All Auto Dealerships Do It

Number 4 on Dr. Nash's list, "reneging or cheating on negotiated terms," deals with not living up to an agreement. Most of us have experienced something similar to the following situation. Bill negotiates a deal with Sam, the salesman, at Charlotte Auto Sales (not the real name) to purchase a nice used Honda Accord for $17,200. As he is about to sign the documents, he notices that Sam has included an additional $150 for administrative fees. When Bill questions the charge, Sam replies, "Oh, that's standard procedure for ordering the title, license, etc., similar to adding taxes. All the dealers do it." At this point, Bill is tired and doesn't want to renegotiate, so he pays the additional charge and completes the transaction. Later, at a social dinner, he relates the event to his friends and learns that several of them have had a similar experience with this dealer. Word gets around, criticizing the dealership and damaging its reputation. People become skeptical and reluctant to do business with Charlotte Auto Sales, particularly with Sam. As a result, business drops off and Sam's commissions decline.

The lesson here? Remember in chapter 4 we discussed episodes documented in an article titled "Personal Values and Business Decisions"? One of the situations discussed involved a firm that dealt unfairly with a customer and lost business as a result. Companies that deal directly with the public must go the extra mile to insure that the customer is treated fairly and is satisfied. One disgruntled customer can damage the good reputation that has taken much time and effort to build.

The Heartbeat of America

Another issue we are often confronted with is poor quality (number 8 on Dr. Nash's list). An example of perceived poor quality is the nationally publicized story of the General Motors customer who took his Oldsmobile Delta 88 to a mechanic for service. The mechanic discovered that the motor was a Chevrolet engine. The story found its way to the mass media, and a flood of negative publicity rose against GM.

Unhappy customers, charging fraud and unethical behavior, filed storms of class action lawsuits. GM, of course, responded that it was common practice to have components made at the most efficient and cost-effective factories regardless of whether or not Oldsmobile owned them. Officials contended that this practice was in the best interest of the consumer because it reduced cost.

In an attempt to put this bad publicity behind them, General Motors eventually settled for a reported $40 million. In reality, this episode cost them more than the amount of the settlement. Incalculable human resource hours and energy were lost fighting the lawsuits and administering damage control. Rather than directing these hours and energy to enhance the interest of GM shareholders, customers, and employees, they were consumed in fighting fires. Also, there's no way to evaluate how many customers were lost or what it cost trying to woo them back.[3] This is further confirmation of the Zetlin study referred to in chapter 4, which found that publicized unethical conduct has a negative effect on companies.

87

Does the End Really Justify the Means?

Do you remember the exposé ABC did on the Food Lion grocery chain in 1996? With hidden cameras and concealed microphones, *Primetime Live* reporters went undercover and worked as employees to investigate allegations that Food Lion was selling spoiled food. The exposé claimed—indeed, proclaimed in living color— that employees repackaged rotting meat, and that old fish were dipped in bleach. *Primetime* also alleged that Food Lion sold fruits and vegetables taken from fly-infested dumpsters and cheese nibbled by rats. According to *Fortune* magazine, after the program aired, Food Lion's market value dropped $1.3 billion, and a decline in revenues and profits forced them to close eighty-four stores and lay off 3,500 employees.[4]

But that wasn't the end of the story. Food Lion filed suit against ABC for $2.47 billion, claiming it had been smeared. The suit charged *Primetime Live* with fraud, trespass, and breach of its fiduciary responsibility. Interestingly, according to *Quill* Magazine, Food Lion's suit was unusual because it didn't contain a libel claim. While Food Lion was zealously defending its reputation with denials of any wrongdoing in the public arena, in court they were contesting the way the information was gathered. In January 1997, the court ordered *ABC News* to pay $5.5 million to Food Lion.[5]

As I read the accounts of this story, the way the information was presented and the way the facts were distorted bewildered me. I couldn't draw any conclusion as to who did right and who did wrong. Did Food Lion really sell food it shouldn't, or did ABC falsify the story? It seems the spin doctors have waved their magic wands and created such misinformation that it's difficult to know the truth. It appears the lawsuit's major claim was that ABC used illegal tactics, deception, and lies to gather its information, not that the information it gathered was false. Well, *I* want to know the truth, but I doubt that the whole truth will ever come out.

In any event, we know that someone, Food Lion or ABC (or maybe both), was involved in deceptive practices, and it has cost a pile of money in actual damages and loss of future revenues. And, as usual in cases like this, the only real winners were the attorneys.

This occurrence has so many convolutions that it's hard to condense the events into one principle. However, it is clear that "serving the public" as defined in the Johnson and Johnson study in chapter 4 was not a primary concern, and the resulting financial damage was devastating.

It's Hard to Drain the Swamp When You're Up to Your Rear End in Alligators

As these three examples highlight, unethical behavior costs money. Maybe not in the short run, but ultimately, it has a high price. If the bad behavior hits the media, its costs can include a damaged reputation, a drop in stock prices, and a loss of sales, all of which affect the bottom line. If the behavior affects another organization, even if it isn't publicized, the offending company's relationship is damaged, and trust is diminished. Also, there could be legal fees and restitution costs, as well as the cost of the time that management spends dealing with the problem.

But even if the unethical acts never see the light of day, the employees are aware of them, and the company suffers in employee loyalty, trust, and commitment to the organization. This translates into higher turnover, less emphasis on quality, and a who-cares attitude.

89

In a survey sponsored by *USA Today*, nearly one-third of 4,035 workers contacted reported that they felt pressured by their firms to violate stated company policy in order to achieve business objectives. Half of the workers said they experienced such pressures regularly. The study also found that nearly one-third of employees had witnessed some form of misconduct they believed had violated either company policy or the law.[6] According to another survey sponsored by the Ethics Officers Association, 47 percent of top executives and 76 percent of M.B.A students were prepared to massage figures in order to make a company's profit appear larger. If the majority of M.B.A. students, our future executives, are willing to falsify reports, the situation isn't going to improve. With statistics such as these, it's disheartening but not surprising that *Psychology Today* found that 48 percent of Americans were actually involved in unethical conduct at work.[7]

You've heard it said that high profits cover a multitude of sins. Well, the reciprocal is also true: reduce the sins and keep the profit that would be used to cover them.

Christopher Fleming

Of course, the premise of this chapter, and of this book, is not only that unethical behavior is costly and eats away profit but that the opposite is also true. Those holding a stake in any organization—suppliers, employees, customers, investors, and the community—respond to high moral ethics and standards with good will, harmony, trust, loyalty, and commitment to the organization. This good will translates into reduced costs, higher quality of the products or services, and a bigger bottom line.

In his book *Managing Corporate Ethics*, Francis J. Aguilar examines the anatomy of a company managed with the kind of morality I'm advocating. He uses the Dover Corporation as his example. Dover is actually a family of companies that manufacture industrial products, including elevators, oil pumps, valves, toggle clamps, flow meters, parking meters, and automobile lifts. Their financial performance has been impressive, with a 15.9 percent return on average equity.

One of the tenets of Dover's management philosophy is a trusting, supportive environment. They believe in being open and honest and in communicating problems as well as numbers not only within each division but also across corporate lines. One subsidiary, Groen, an old-line food processing manufacturer, found itself in an industry where consultants were used to advise the clients which products to buy. Some of the consultants expected manufacturing companies to pay them a commission for specifying their equipment. Although the practice wasn't illegal, it was unethical. Too often, the company who paid the most commissions was specified the most. Groen refused to pay this commission. Louise O'Sullivan, Groen's president, said, "If we start to do unethical acts in one part of our business, it sends out a strong signal that people can play games in other parts. . . . This would destroy the fabric of this company. We depend so much on being able to trust each other." Being able to share the problem with other Dover managers gave O'Sullivan the confidence to do what she felt was right.

Dover's divisions and subsidiaries share their problems with each other openly instead of keeping them confidential, as most of us were taught to do. This openness benefits everybody. With luck, someone else has experienced a similar problem and can offer a solution or at least act as a sounding board to explore options. A second benefit of this kind of communication is that people enjoy the support of their fellow managers; they don't feel they are alone. A third benefit is that all employees have a clear understanding of how their division and the overall organization are doing. They share problems as well as opportunities, communicating information in all directions, up and down the management ladder and from one division to another. This provides a catalyst for problem solving and opportunity development. A fourth benefit of this trusting environment is that it provides division management with the freedom to do what is right without the fear of "corporate" cutting you loose if things don't work out.[8]

Would You Buy a Used Car from This Man?

Remember Sam, the auto salesman? He finally left Charlotte Auto Sales because his sales had declined to the point where he could no longer make a living. Sam heard of a new dealership in town that was doing very well, and he decided to apply.

His interview was with John, the sales manager, who belonged to the same church as Sam. Years before, Sam had joined the largest Baptist church in town because he thought it would be a good place to make contacts and because he felt that being a church member would be good for business. John, on the other hand, was a committed Christian and conducted his business activities accordingly.

John explained to Sam that auto salesmen in the area had a less-than-admirable reputation. They were perceived (by the town) as being interested only in the commission, not in serving the customer. People were suspicious of the stereotypical car salesman; a persistent, high-pressure haggler who would say anything to make the sale. Buyers believed that if they weren't very careful, they would wind up with something unreliable that they didn't want.

John explained that this dealership operated under a different concept. All salespeople would be salaried, no commissions. All used cars would go through a diagnostic check and be completely reconditioned before being offered for sale. There also would be no haggling. The price listed would be both fair and final.

John continued to explain that the business would be run on high ethical principles, and its mission was, "To be the most responsive and customer-oriented organization possible."

The values the company embraced were:

- Have customer-focused processes that inform and empower the customers and allow them to make an informed choice.
- Provide unparalleled selection of fully certified cars and trucks, supported by exceptional warranty.
- Present a consultative, nonmanipulative, friendly environment. The foundation commitment is to provide a place characterized by truth and trust.[9]

After much deliberation and soul searching, the company decided to give Sam a chance. John, being a Christian, felt that if Sam could make the transition to a different ethical orientation and be an asset to the business in the long run, then John should make the commitment of time and energy to train him. Sam was hired on probation and given specific guidelines to help him meet the required standards.

Sam made some mistakes, like telling one customer that a particular car had low mileage because the previous owner had been an elderly lady. Her husband had died and she was left with two cars, and she alternated driving them. The truth was that the car had been confiscated in a drug sting and had been sitting in a police lot for two years. John was patient about these lapses. He gently corrected Sam and explained the necessity of being honest; then he ordered Sam to go to the customer and tell the truth. John also lovingly told Sam that if he lied again to a customer, he would be fired.

This story is based on the operating principles of Driver's Mart, a company founded in Dearborn, Michigan in 1996. Capitalizing on the dubious reputation of the used car industry, Driver's Mart provided an ethical choice for the buyer. The customer could relax, knowing that there would be no hassles, the price listed would be the final price, and what the salesperson said would be the truth. The vehicles had been inspected and were sound, and the dealership would stand behind the warranty. Today the Driver's Mart organization enjoys over twenty-five locations in six states and is growing at a rate that Wal-Mart would envy. More importantly, it is recognized as having a positive impact on the whole automotive industry.[10]

Summary

The examples I have given in this chapter are real, or they represent a real situation. They are the stuff that corporate life is made of. We are exposed to these kinds of situations every day. We see it all around us, in the papers, on the six o'clock news, and closer to home, in our offices and places of business.

When you are faced with these decisions—I've heard them called moments of truth—I hope you are convinced that there are long-term benefits to taking the high moral road. Not only are there the emotional benefits of a clear conscience and peace of mind, but also there are the practical benefits of having a more successful operation and making more money.

I don't believe that doing the right thing will always lead directly to financial success, or that unethical behavior will always be disastrous. However, this I do believe: Over time, a pattern of operating a business by the Golden Rule—treat others as you would want them to treat you—will lead to better relationships with all stakeholders. This ethical stance will cause your organization to be more financially successful than you will be if you engage in a pattern of deceptive and selfish practices.

In Psalm 73, David mused about why men who he knew were dishonest were so successful and had such a life of ease. He complained, "Have I been wasting my time? Why take the trouble to be pure? All I get out of it is trouble and woe." David must have been having a real bad day. Later in that same psalm, he realized how ridiculous his statement was and concluded, "What a slippery path they are on—suddenly God will send them sliding over the edge of a cliff and down to their destruction: an instant end to all their happiness, an eternity of terror. Their present life is only a dream! They will awaken to the truth as one awakens from a dream of things that never really were!"[11] David, as revealed in some of his other writings, had been there, done that, and had seen the results. Like David, we can learn from other people's experiences or from our own. I've done some of both.

7

I'm Ethical . . . Right?

*It has been my experience that folks who
have no vices have very few virtues.*

Abraham Lincoln

How would you feel if the president of the company that you worked for, or were on the board of directors of, had been or was accused of

- having an affair with a young lady that worked for the company,
- making unwanted advances toward other ladies working in his office,
- using his office to influence a supplier to loan money to a business venture he had been involved in,
- raising money illegally,

- influencing other people to lie about these allegations,
- inflating profits to deceive investors?

And, to add salt to the wound, the president was using company funds to pay attorney fees and spin doctors to defend himself in these investigations.

I hope that if you were in a position to do something about this situation, you would use your authority, or whatever influence you had, to remove this person from his position until these issues were resolved.

Unfortunately, this kind of scenario is being played out all over America—in boardrooms and in political offices. And that's disturbing for several reasons. First, spin doctors have too often shifted the focus from right and wrong and used verbal smoke screens to obscure the real issue. Second, I'm even more disturbed that we, as Americans, don't seem to care anymore that our corporate and political leaders often fail to conduct their personal lives with the same integrity we would expect from our spouse or business associates. I'm not saying that most leaders are guilty of these kinds of things; I'm concerned that the American people don't seem to care if they *are* guilty! Where's the outrage? Where are the calls for an end to irresponsible and unethical leadership?

What does this say to our children about values? Don't we want our kids to grow up with the good values that made America strong? Don't we want to return to the time when a person's "yes" meant yes and "no" meant no—where their word was their bond? We don't want our children to have situational ethics, morals that change according to how the situation affects them. You can't have it both ways: leaders who conduct themselves immorally and kids who have a good value system. Children look up to and emulate our leaders. Of course, you want your kids to develop high standards of integrity and a strong sense of right and wrong. You want them to have that internal compass that points them in the right direction when they find themselves in unfamiliar territory. Well, doesn't it follow that the leaders of organizations (corporate and governmental), people whom your children *will* admire and emulate, should be above reproach?

Why don't we do something about the unethical behavior of our business and governmental officials? Here's the reason. I have heard that if you put a frog in a pan of boiling water, it will probably jump out. But if you put the frog in cool water and slowly raise the temperature, it will not jump out before the heat paralyzes it. It will die because the change is gradual. Well, I believe that if we aren't diligent in investigating wrongdoing, we become apathetic toward it. If we don't pursue the truth and hold our leaders accountable for their behavior, personal as well as professional, their conduct will reflect our indifference. If there is no outrage when those in authority are caught doing wrong, then their standards will degenerate into situational ethics, ethics that depend on their perspective at the time. As a result, our tolerance for unethical behavior among our leaders, both governmental and corporate, will continue to increase. Ladies and gentlemen, the temperature of acceptance of immorality in America is rising, and we had better take action before, like the frog, we are paralyzed by the gradual change. Before it is too late to do anything about it.

America, Where Is Your Moral Compass?

You may have heard of a book titled *The Day America Told the Truth*. This book is the result of surveys conducted by James Patterson and Peter Kim to "unearth and quantify the personal ethics, values, and beliefs" of Americans. The surveys revealed some shocking information about the temperature of our value system:

> Sure enough, money talked to people across the country. For $10 million, one in four of us would abandon all of our friends or abandon our church. About as many would turn to prostitution for a week. Some of us would go much farther—as far as murder, changing their race, or a sex-change operation. In fact, 7 percent of us would murder someone for money. That's about one in every fourteen people. Whether they could actually pull the trigger is another question, but 36 million of us would be willing to consider the offer. . . . The results remained pretty much the same at $5 million, at $4 million, and at $3 million.

Two million dollars is where there is a fall-off in what people were willing to do. According to Patterson and Kim, "Our price in America seems to be two million or thereabouts." [1]

The Law of Precedence

How does this moral decay relate to business? Here's how! A poll commissioned by Hyatt Hotels & Resorts indicated that one-third of people who confessed to cheating at golf (personal) also admitted to cheating at the office (professional). [2] I'm saying that businesses are made up of people, and that corporations assume the ethics of their leaders and their employees. A wise friend once said, "People make a business what it is. Everything else can be bought in a hardware store."

The primary moral guide for businesspeople today is what I call *the law of precedence*. This is not a codified law of the land. It is generally accepted unethical business practices. It says an act is accepted as okay, even though it skirts the law, if it can be done without significant legal problems or without being condemned by customers, employees, vendors, or stockholders. Or if it can be done without anyone finding out. Webster Hubble, in his now famous taped prison conversations with his wife, gave an example of this law. He was talking about attorneys overbilling clients when he said, "All lawyers do it," implying that it's okay because it complies with the law of precedence.

As I said earlier, my standards of morality haven't always been high. I'm sorry for that. However, because of my lack of a good value system in my early professional life, I was exposed to unhealthy situations and have personal knowledge of several real examples that illustrate my point.

Owen Industrial Supply (not its real name), an industrial equipment supply company, had a large number of small vendors from which it purchased materials. Management set out on a growth strategy of acquiring small competitors in the surrounding area. In order to help finance the growth, the company extended its payables from the 30-day terms, to which it had previously agreed with its vendors, to between 60 and 120-day terms. Because most of its vendors were small and Owen represented a large portion of their business, most had no choice but to accept the extension, and Owen was successful in financing the program. Most of us in the corporate world have seen companies that allowed payables to slide beyond the supplier's terms.

Johnson & Associates (not its real name) is a large holding company with tens of thousands of employees. Although its interests are wide and varied, most of its holdings are affected in some way by the decisions made by high-level state and federal officials. In order to influence these politicians, Johnson would require its employees to contribute to the political campaigns of candidates it thought it could influence. One notable campaign was for a high government office. In this campaign, some of the employees were not only asked to contribute to Johnson's choice of candidates, but because of the significance of the office, they were asked to contribute sizable sums, which were reimbursed through expense reports. When Johnson's candidate won the election, the elected official's people were so grateful that Johnson was allowed to select the head of the agency that provided funding for many of its activities. Have you ever felt job pressure to contribute to or vote for a political candidate?

What Ethics Ain't

I'm not talking about whether lawyers should solicit accident victims as clients or whether doctors should charge for their time even if they misdiagnose a medical problem. You have heard it said that "among reasonable men there is room for disagreement," and these disagreements do occur, as the following illustrations attest.

An appliance store salesperson doesn't include the electrical connection in her installation bid because she assumes that the customer knows that state codes require that a licensed electrician do the electrical work. Yet the customer thinks it should have been included. This is an honest misunderstanding.

Or an automobile repair shop doesn't include the dent in the rear fender in his bid to repair the front bumper, but the car owner assumes that it had been factored into the estimate. These issues are not ethical in nature; they are perception and communication problems.

102

Ethics is a system of beliefs about what is right and what is wrong. Each of us has a set of beliefs, but it varies from person to person. For example, one person believes in capital punishment and another person, with the same information but with a different belief system, feels capital punishment is wrong. However, while individual value systems differ, cultural systems are remarkably similar. Ralph Linton, who researched cultural morals, found that value systems don't vary significantly from culture to culture. A comparative study of a large number of cultures indicates that the basic values of most societies include many of the same elements.[3]

C. S. Lewis, the British author and moral philosopher, agreed with Linton. He said, "In general, the morals of all societies are similar. Although they disagree over some points, behavior such as selfishness and deceitfulness are universally unacceptable." Lewis made two additional points: "Human beings, all over the earth, have this curious idea that they ought to behave in a certain way, and can't really get rid of it."[4] Lewis goes on to say that even though people know how to behave, they don't always do what they know is right.

Linton and Lewis confirm my research that there are objective universal principles that govern the ethics of societies. The problem is, as individuals, we don't adhere to them.

Living with a conscience is like driving a car with the brakes on.

Bud Schulberg

A Working Definition

What are ethics, and how would we define them? I subscribe to utilitarian ethics, a term first coined by David Hume, an eighteenth-century Scottish philosopher, and later refined by John Stuart Mill, a nine-teenth-century Englishman and member of Parliament. Utilitarianism, or the Greatest Happiness principle, "holds that actions are right in proportion as they tend to promote happiness, wrong as they tend to promote the reverse."[5] To restate in modern English, ethics is a system of beliefs, which when acted upon leads to the greatest benefit for the most people. I would also add to this definition the words of the Hippocratic oath as espoused by several management gurus, "Above all, do no harm."

Fuzzy Values Equals Fuzzy Ethics

As we have discussed, the term "values" has differ-ent meanings to different people. We all have a set of values, and these values are the foundation for our sys-tem of beliefs. We formulate them from our family, friends, and experiences, and these values have no independent existence other than within each of us. They are unique to the individual. Hitler, Mussolini, and Jeffrey Dahmer all had a set of values. Hitler, for example, believed that the Aryan race was superior to other races. He also believed that there was no good or evil, truth or falsehood, and that whoever amassed the most power was right. He didn't believe in ab-solutes or that there were foundational principles that cut across cultural lines and that stood the test of time. His Golden Rule was, He who has the gold makes the rule.

Many people believe that there are no absolutes. Why shouldn't they? As stated in the first part of this chapter, our leaders certainly don't adhere to any consistent eth-ical code. And when they are called to account for their behavior, they fall back on "everyone does it" or "I didn't violate any laws" or "that's a personal issue, and doesn't have anything to do with my professional duties."

Given this legal environment where it's all about strategy, not what's right or wrong, it's no wonder Americans believe there are no absolutes and that everything is relative. When they are confronted with an issue that requires a moral decision, they draw on their experiences. Logic leads them to respond based on the best strategy and how it will affect them, not how it will affect others. Their value system dictates that they appraise the situation, then evaluate what action is to be taken based on the greatest benefit to them. That's what our leaders, through their actions, advocate.

The movie *Grease* illustrates my point that our behavior is relative to our situation, and that people (the audience) accept the plot as "just the way people are." In the beginning of the movie, John Travolta was trying to convince Olivia Newton-John he was a nice guy by not revealing his true personality. He believed their relationship was a summer affair, and he wouldn't see her again after the summer was over. He deceived her by pretending to be someone he really wasn't. Then, as luck would have it, she was transferred to his school the following fall and ran into him. He got caught in the deception, and the truth came out. Of course, in the movie everything works out. In real life, however, it often doesn't, and we have to accept the consequences of our actions. Some of them have a lasting effect.

Yes, There Are Absolutes

Unlike the people who believe that everything is relative, I'm convinced that there are absolutes. There are principles that are true, timeless, and always right, regardless of the situation. I believe that these principles should be the foundation of our belief system and our individual values, and that the values of our society should reflect them. Thomas Aquinas wrote, "Without morals, there can be no law."

W. T. Stace said, "All men, because of their common humanity, have certain universal needs in common. There is only one way of satisfying those needs and that way is the same for all men. It is the way of morality."[6] Without a principles-based value system underpinning our laws and, more importantly, our actions, we will be stunted as individuals, and we won't be able to trust our neighbor enough to function as a business or a society.

Since I'm writing on ethics, I might as well be upfront and say that I believe these "absolutes" are God-given and can be found in the Judeo-Christian Bible. However, they can also be found in the writings of Plato, Aristotle, Confucius, and other philosophers who were known for their logic rather than for their religion. Curiously, the majority of ancient philosophers, including those I just mentioned, assumed that morality was divinely given, that God ordained the rules an individual, and thus a society, should live by. Only after the sixteenth century did men begin looking for a humanistic origin for core morality.

According to these and other great thinkers, the basic reasons for having moral fundamentals are to avoid causing harm to others and to promote the greatest happiness for the greatest number of people. Interestingly, these great thinkers all subscribed to the same set of absolutes. This may account for their belief that the "laws" were divinely given. They also believed that absolutes have two characteristics: (1) rational men can understand them, and (2) they would have the same benefits for any society.[7]

Where Do Values Come From?

Where *do* an individual's values come from? Are they divinely given or developed through human experience? Let me reiterate that there is a difference between a person's values and true morality, as it is generally understood. As I have already said, everyone has a set of values (ethics), but because they differ from individual to individual, they may not be what society considers worthwhile, praiseworthy, or right.

Richard Brandt, in his book *Ethical Theory*, synthesized the theories of some of the best psychologists of his day into a theory to which I subscribe. He concluded that an individual's values were developed in three stages.

1. Home Influences: Studies show that the views of siblings about issues that involve ethical questions are correlated . . . and the same is true of the views of children and their parents.
2. Peer Groups: As the child grows older, the parent's reputation for omniscience tends to decline. . . . The view of scientists, philosophers, and others— or more likely, the opinions of the child's peer group, or the opinion he (or she) attributes to the community or nation—will tend to be accepted as authoritative.
3. As the child matures, the adult values are influenced by personal experiences and by the intellectual necessity for having a coherent structure of beliefs.[8]

It's easy (and logical) to understand that a child raised in a strict moral environment—family and community— will tend to be ethical, but a child raised without strong moral influences will tend to develop coping mechanisms that are different from accepted moral behavior.

According to the great philosophers, a society's moral structure derives from the necessity to protect its members. As I have already said, the basic reasons for having moral fundamentals in a society are to avoid causing harm to others and to promote the greatest happiness for the greatest number of people.

Summary

When 7 percent of us would consider killing someone for $2 million, I think we can conclude that America has lost its moral orientation. This disorientation also carries over into our business activities. The prevailing moral guide among a significant percentage of our corporations is not what is right but what is the law, what is the punishment if we get caught, and have other companies gotten away with it? Corporations are just groups of people. They assume the ethics of the leadership and the individuals who run them.

Everyone has a set of values, and this set forms the basis of his or her ethics. However, these values are unique to the individual and may not be the same as those that society holds as right. Jeffrey Dahmer had a value system, but it certainly differed from your and my beliefs. America needs to reestablish its value system using the absolutes that made our country great. Our children need to be taught these absolutes and our leaders, both political and corporate, must be held accountable to them. Only when we, as a nation, embrace and enforce the moral absolutes as our code of ethics will we stop the moral relativity dance done by our attorneys and spin doctors and return to the days where a person's word is his bond and business is done with a handshake.

PART 3

NAVIGATING
THE CORPORATE
MINEFIELD

The first responsibility of any corporate citizen

"was spelled out clearly 2,500 years ago, in the

Hippocratic oath of the Greek physician:

'primum non nocere: *above all,*

not knowingly to do harm.'"

Peter Drucker

8

ARE THERE ABSOLUTES?
ABSOLUTELY!

*If you don't know where you are going, any
road will take you.*

Now that we have discussed what morality means
and where it comes from, let's bite into the core
issue. What are the absolutes, the core values
or fundamental morals that don't change with time or
situation?

In preparation for his book *Shared Values in a Troubled World,* Rushworth Kidder asked people around the
world, "If you could help create a global code of ethics,
what would it be?" Compiling the answers, he found the
code would consist of the following: love, truthfulness,
fairness, freedom, unity, tolerance, responsibility, and
respect for life.[1]

Kidder's research confirms the codified ethics of the major religions. According to theologian Hans Kung, all great religions have five basic moral tenets.

1. Do not kill.
2. Do not lie.
3. Do not steal.
4. Do not practice immorality.
5. Respect parents and love children.[2]

Another moral precept that has endured and cuts across philosophical and religious boundaries is the Golden Rule. Confucius said, "What you yourself do not want, do not do to another person."[3] The moral philosopher Immanuel Kant endorses the rule this way, "So act as to treat humanity, whether in thine own person or in that of any other . . . as an end withal, never as means only."[4]

The Golden Rule is also commanded by all the major religions. Buddhism states it this way, "A state that is not pleasing or delightful to me, how could I inflict that upon another?"[5] In Hinduism, it's, "Do naught unto others which would cause you pain if done to you."[6] Islam has, "Not one of you is a believer until he loves for his brother what he loves for himself."[7] In Judaism, it's, "Do not do to others what you would not want them to do to you."[8] In Christianity, "So in everything, do to others what you would have them do to you."[9]

Using the above and other research as my authority, I have concluded that the core absolutes germane to our discussion are those found in the ancient religions as codified by the Jewish Talmud and the Christian Bible:

1. Don't murder.
2. Don't commit adultery.
3. Don't steal.

4. Don't deceive.
5. Don't covet.
6. Whatever you want people to do for you, do also for them.

There are five other moral laws in the Talmud: "Honor your mother and father; have no other god before me; don't make or worship idols; don't misuse the Lord's name, and keep the Sabbath holy." However, these don't have implications in secular interpersonal relationships and are not germane to our discussion.[10]

Why should you, as an individual, strive to be moral and adopt these core values as your ethics? Aristotle said it best, "Morality is a means to an end. Happiness is that end. . . . Yes, happiness is the end we all strive for."[11] One of the foundations of happiness is a good character, and morality is foundational to a good character. We will discuss this premise in detail in the following chapters.

You Don't Need a Road Map, You Need a Compass

What are the characteristics of an ethical business-person, and how do these core values relate to the Monday morning real world when you are up to your rear end in alligators? The best way I know to communicate this is to give you a description of a person who possesses these characteristics. Let's look at the conclusions of people who have done exhaustive studies in this area.

Dr. Stephen Covey, author of *The Seven Habits of Highly Effective People*, defines eight "discernible characteristics of people who are principled leaders." I would add that these qualities also apply to people who want to become leaders.

- They are continually learning. They continually expand their competence and their ability to do things.
- They are service oriented. They must have a sense of responsibility, of service, of contribution.
- They radiate positive energy. Their attitude is optimistic, positive, and upbeat.
- They believe in other people. They believe in the unseen potential of all people.
- They lead balanced lives. They read . . . and keep up with current affairs and events. They are active socially, . . . intellectually, . . . and physically.
- They see life as an adventure. Principle-centered people savor life. Because their security comes from within instead of from without, they have no need to categorize and stereotype everything and everybody.
- They are synergistic. They improve almost any situation they get into.
- They exercise for self-renewal. They exercise the four dimensions of the human personality: physical, mental, emotional, and spiritual.[12]

Another set of defining characteristics comes from Father Raymond Baumhart, who conducted a groundbreaking research project in 1968 that is still relevant today. This project produced one of the most exhaustive studies of businesspersons' attitudes and responses that has been conducted, even to this day. His research yielded the following composite of the ethical business professional:

- Either through childhood influences, college training, or other sources, they have developed the conviction that it is important to act ethically.

- They have a single standard of behavior at home and at work.
- They work for a company with a deserved reputation for integrity.
- They believe that good ethics is good business in the long run.[13]

The father of management, Dr. Peter Drucker, offered another characteristic of the ethical businessperson, whom he called "a professional." As I quoted earlier, he, among others, believes the first responsibility of any corporate citizen "was spelled out clearly 2,500 years ago, in the Hippocratic oath of the Greek physician: *'primum non nocere:* above all, not knowingly to do harm.'"[14]

The above descriptions, and others uncovered during my research, have confirmed my observations of the character of a moral and ethical businessperson. Synthesizing this investigation with my own experience with people who were successful in motivating others and getting the job done yielded the following description of ethical businesspeople:

1. They will be consistently honest, fair, and impartial in all of their dealings, regardless of the behavior of the other parties involved.
2. They will not be party to unfair, unethical, unhealthy, or unlawful activities.
3. They are sensitive to the feelings, needs, and impediments of fellow team members.
4. They are loyal to fellow team members. They don't talk behind their backs; they are supportive and *primum non nocere.*
5. They are distinguished by the following personal values:

- Under no circumstances do they deceive.
- They do not steal—money or paper clips.
- They are accurate and precise in all transactions.
- They keep their word.
- They aren't jealous of their coworkers' successes.

In addition to these attributes, people of integrity *treat others as they would want others to treat them.* Sound familiar?

The Road to Ethics

Business ethics aren't only a list of dos and don'ts. They also include policies that promote the Golden Rule among all stakeholders:

- Treating employees with respect, being honest with them, and empowering them.
- Working with customers and suppliers; encouraging teamwork and doing what is promised.
- Fulfilling the moral obligation of responsible corporate citizenship in the community.

An example of corporate good citizenship was Levi Strauss's decision to drop 5 percent of its contractors and mandate improvements in another 25 percent to insure that acceptable human rights practices were followed in undeveloped countries. Don't you agree that this was a painful decision?

As I stated earlier, organizations are just groups of people. In order for a company to be a workplace of high integrity where people enjoy the benefits of an ethical, fair, and pleasant environment, the people that make up

116

the company—both the leadership and its employees—must themselves have integrity. A code of ethics and a mission statement that is adhered to can do a lot to foster an ethical corporation. But as Chuck Colson said in a speech to the Harvard Business School students, "The line between good and evil passes not between principalities and powers, but it oscillates within the human heart."[15]

We all have heard of the term "gang mentality," which refers to a group of individuals taking on a collective mentality. The same phenomenon occurs within an organization, where members of a team often develop a group identity, a corporate personality. New employees are especially susceptible to this syndrome, particularly if the company is highly respected and successful. Wanting to fit in, they seek the approval of their superiors and peers by submerging themselves in the corporate environment.

At Rockwell Manufacturing, a company I had the privilege of working for in the early seventies, I experienced a very *good* group mentality. The management, and consequently the employees, were supportive and caring. If the people had been self-centered, suspicious, and had a look-out-for-number-one mentality, I would have assumed the same attitude and not enjoyed my time there. But because it was such an unselfish, supportive atmosphere, I did enjoy the experience, and it contributed to my present belief in the value of ethics.

Not all organizations have the high ethical standards I enjoyed at Rockwell. All of us have known companies that promote unethical behavior among the employees in an attempt to maximize profit—companies where management fosters unhealthy competition to keep all its employees on their toes and giving maximum effort, and where squeezing customers and suppliers for "a little bit extra" is the *modus operandi*.

For an employee to sleep at night, he or she must have a personal moral system that is compatible with the organization's principles—and he or she must be true to them. If your values truly conflict with those of the organization, you need to leave. Otherwise you will be continually frustrated, you won't be able to give 100 percent loyalty to the enterprise, and you certainly won't be comfortable working in that culture.

Summary

Are there absolutes that apply to the secular world? Yes! They are:

1. Don't murder.
2. Don't commit adultery.
3. Don't steal.
4. Don't deceive.
5. Don't covet.
6. Treat others as you would want them to treat you.

Why should you, as an individual, strive to be moral and adopt these core values as your ethics? Aristotle said it best: "Morality is a means to an end. Happiness is that end." Yes, happiness is the end we all strive for. One of the foundations of happiness is a good character, and morality is foundational to a good character.

9

I WISH EVERYONE WERE
AS RIGHTEOUS AS I

*In order to preserve your self respect, it's
sometimes necessary to lie and cheat.*

Robert Byrne

Are you ethical? Of course you are. My ethics are
the highest; they are just and correct. Everyone
should have the same value system as I. Sonin,
my wife, is ethical also! Of course, her ethics aren't quite
up to my standards, but she does okay. Unfortunately,
we're the only ones with the right ethics. Everyone else's
system is flawed. And, as the old saying goes, I'm beginning to worry about her.

We all have a set of ethics, and each of us is loyal to
our own values. However, each individual's value sys-

tem varies and is, to some degree, different from the norm of society. This variation is normally small and has a lot to do with our opinion of the reasonableness of a particular rule or law. For example, one person may feel that a speed limit is too low and decide to violate it. Most of us have at least considered this. However, in the game of business, because business is teamwork, if the team is pulling in different directions, these differences can have significant consequences.

Here is an example of such differing ethics. Several years ago, we hired a young man to work on one of Pioneer's assembly lines. Dan (not his real name) was a good employee in every respect. He was honest, cheerful, and got along well with everyone. He was industrious and conscientious in all of his responsibilities while at work—just an all-around good employee. But there was this one problem. He habitually missed an average of four days per month. Since he was paid on an hourly basis, not only did his absence affect the company, but it also affected his income. Because he was a model employee in every other area, his supervisor, Jack, tolerated the problem even when other employees complained that they had to work around Dan's schedule. Although Jack didn't want to lose him, the situation became intolerable. Not only was it beginning to affect production, but also we were stretching our own employment rules by allowing him to miss so much work.

After the warning process had been exhausted, the day finally came when Jack had to release Dan. In the exit interview, Jack asked him why he was so responsible in all areas except attendance; why did he only work an average of four days a week? Dan looked away for a moment, pondering his answer, then with a grin looked back at Jack and said, "Because I can't make ends meet on three days a week."

120

Dan's value system required him to give 100 percent while he was on the job, but it didn't include working five days a week. That would be acceptable had he and Jack agreed to this schedule when Dan was hired, but the agreement was that he would be at work during office hours five days a week. His value system not only conflicted with this company's rules but with accepted business practices. This chapter is dedicated to helping you compare your value system to the moral principles (absolutes) developed in the last chapter and to recalibrate your moral compass to true north, if need be.

In chapter 6, we discussed a list of ethical quandaries developed by Dr. Laura Nash. Our research indicates that although this list isn't exhaustive, it is representative of unethical behavior found in the workplace. Now let's look at these acts through a different set of eyes, sorted according to the principle each violates. We found in the last chapter that there are six moral absolutes that apply to our discussion. Four of these apply both to Dr. Nash's activities and to business in general. They are: don't deceive, don't steal, don't covet, and treat others as you would want them to treat you. Here is Dr. Nash's list of quandaries sorted according to each principle.

Unethical Behavior and the Principle It Violates

Deceiving	Misleading product or service claims.
	Failing to speak up when unethical practices occur.
	Making a product that perpetrates a questionable safety issue.
	Knowingly exaggerating the advantages of a plan in order to get needed support.
	Promoting the destructive go-getter who outruns his mistakes.
	Lying by omission to employees for the sake of the business.
	Not taking responsibility for injurious practices—intentional or not.
	Cover-ups and misrepresentations in reporting and control procedures.

121

Stealing	Producing inferior quality.
	Reneging or cheating on negotiated terms.
	Not putting back what you take out of the environment, employees, and/or corporate assets.
	Courting the corporate hierarchy versus doing the job well.
	Not paying within terms.
	Abusing or going along with questionable corporate perks.
	Corrupting the political process through legal means.
Mistreating Others	Establishing policy that is likely to cause others to lie to get the job done.
	Overconfidence in one's own judgment to the risk of the corporate entity.
	Humiliating people at work or by stereotypes in advertising.
	Favoritism.
	Sacrificing the innocent and helpless in order to accomplish the objective.
	Suppression of basic rights: freedom of speech, of choice, and of personal relationships.
	Failing to address bigotry, sexism, or racism.
	Failing to cooperate with other areas of the company—the enemy mentality.
	Knowingly making an alliance with a questionable partner, albeit for a good cause.
	Disloyalty to the company as soon as times get tough.
	Climbing the corporate ladder by stepping on others.
Coveting	Self-aggrandizement over corporate obligations.
	Greed.
	Lockstep obedience to authority, however unethical and unfair it may be.[1]

Sorting these acts by the injunction they violate confirms the authority of the moral principles and simplifies the research process.

In conducting our research to correlate ethics to profits, we created forty-two vignettes that represented most of these unethical activities. We planned to use them to measure the ethics of the business community. In order to validate the vignettes' ability to accurately gauge the questionnaire's reliability, a panel of clergy and professional people with credentials qualifying them to evaluate the vignettes was assembled. This panel was asked to rate each question for its correlation with one of the four ethical injunctions. Twenty-four were identified that most closely measured the four principles and offered differentiation between each. Using these to develop a new questionnaire (shown below), we then surveyed the executives of publicly held corporations and correlated the results to their five-year financial performance.

We have already covered the results in chapter 4. My objective here is to share with you the survey questionnaire and allow you to review it (to take it if you like) and ponder how you would react to the situations.

Here are the instructions.

- If you totally agree with the action, circle number 1.
- If you agree with the action, circle number 2.
- If you are neutral, circle number 3.
- If you disagree with the action taken, circle number 4.
- If you strongly disagree with the action, circle number 5.

(The results of this questionnaire are given at the end of this chapter.)

1. Supply and Demand

A panicked customer calls. He has a machine out of service, which has shut his plant down. The machine needs a special part that you have in stock. Because of the uniqueness of the situation, the sales manager suggests adding an additional 20 percent to the price.

Strongly agree   1   2   3   4   5   Strongly disagree

2. Whose Money?

A company builds a unique machine for a customer on a cost-plus basis. Six months after the job is complete, the accounting department informs the salesperson that the materials supplier has given a 10 percent volume rebate on materials, some of which were used on this job. The general manager's position is that the company is entitled to keep the money and not rebate the customer.

Strongly agree   1   2   3   4   5   Strongly disagree

3. We All Make Mistakes

Six months after the year-end inventory, it is discovered that a substantial amount of inventory was inadvertently not counted. Because the company showed adequate profits, the accounting department decided to ignore the additional profit and not report it to the IRS.

Strongly agree   1   2   3   4   5   Strongly disagree

4. The Big Freeze

After a particular employee's raise had been approved, it became known the company's performance had not been as good as projected. The president announced there would be no raises until further notice. Since the raise was submitted before the announcement, the boss decides that the employee can add two hundred dollars per month to his (or her) expense account until the freeze is lifted.

Strongly agree   1   2   3   4   5   Strongly disagree

124

5. The Insurance Dilemma

A company provides health insurance for its employees and their families. Because of an unusually high number of accidents, the insurance carrier has announced a substantial increase in its rates. This increase will materially affect operating profits and adversely affect the company's stock price. After a series of exhausting meetings to consider options, the insurance committee (created to study the problem) recommends that the company raise salaries by the amount of the present insurance premiums and have the employees find their own insurance, even though a few are probably not insurable through individual policies.

Strongly agree   1   2   3   4   5   Strongly disagree

6. Involuntary Retirement

The chairman of an investment company directs the president to purchase control of a small publicly held manufacturing company. He reasons, "I don't like the CEO of that firm and would welcome the opportunity to ask him to retire."

Strongly agree   1   2   3   4   5   Strongly disagree

7. The Old Trojan Horse

An engineer tried unsuccessfully to develop a new product with features similar to those of a competitor's model. Finally, posing as a potential vendor, he goes to the competitor and asks for a set of design specifications to use to "develop a bid" for one of its components. Using the competitor's information, he is able to complete his design.

Strongly agree   1   2   3   4   5   Strongly disagree

8. You Won't Upstage Me!

A sales manager has discovered that the company's principal competitor has rented a large display space at an upcoming trade show in the city where he lives. He requests an increase in his display budget for this particular show because he doesn't want to be upstaged in his own town.

Strongly agree   1   2   3   4   5   Strongly disagree

9. Image Is Everything

The president of a publicly traded, national company reports to his board: "Although the research indicates that going international at this time is not economically justified, I recommend we go ahead with our plans because being an international company will add to our prestige."

Strongly agree   1   2   3   4   5   Strongly disagree

10. Bigger Is Better

The president of a medium-sized, publicly held company tells the sales manager to make sales growth a top priority: "Lower your prices 10 percent if you have to. I want this company to be the largest company in this industry, even if profits have to be sacrificed to do it."

Strongly agree   1   2   3   4   5   Strongly disagree

11. Squeeze the Competition

A marketing strategist reports to the company's marketing department: "The market for this product is mature and not growing. If you want to maximize profits, I recommend that we lower the price and drive the competition out of the market. Then we can raise the price significantly. This strategy will result in the greatest return in the long run."

Strongly agree   1   2   3   4   5   Strongly disagree

12. I'm More Important Than You Are

The division vice president fills his secretarial position by transferring the production manager's administrative assistant over the manager's objections. His logic is that "this lady is the best administrator we have and I want her skills in my office," even though her value to the company is greater with her current position.

Strongly agree   1   2   3   4   5   Strongly disagree

13. Steal the Order

A saleslady tells her sales manager, "We are going to lose this order; our competition at the ABC Company has underbid us." The sales manager responds, "Bid whatever it takes to keep them from getting it. I don't want them to have it, even if we lose money on it."

Strongly agree   1   2   3   4   5   Strongly disagree

14. It's Standard Procedure

An automobile dealership controller recommends to management that they add a handling charge for ordering the title, license, etc. (things they do anyway) to the final bill, as a way to improve profits. "This would not have to be discussed in the initial negotiations," he proposes, "and if it's questioned, we tell the customer that it's standard procedure, like adding taxes. All the dealers do it."

Strongly agree   1   2   3   4   5   Strongly disagree

15. Profits Come First

A saleslady is informed by her sales manager that her customer's order will be delayed because the products that were intended for that customer are being used to fill an order with more profit. He tells her that the higher profit sale is needed to meet the month's profit projections.

Strongly agree   1   2   3   4   5   Strongly disagree

16. Made in America (Not)

A construction contract calls for all materials to be made in America. A painting subcontractor couldn't purchase the specified paint domestically, so rather than delay the job, he decides to purchase a Canadian paint that he feels exceeds the requirements. He reasons, "When it's dry, no one can tell the difference, and this paint will perform better."

Strongly agree   1   2   3   4   5   Strongly disagree

17. We'll Have It Ready, No Problem

An automotive repair shop advertises its policy of completing repairs within one week. But because of an unusually high number of repairs, the average completion time is now up to twelve days. The manager tells his staff: "If the customers ask, tell them it may take a little longer but try to avoid giving a specific date. If they don't ask, don't volunteer one."

Strongly agree   1   2   3   4   5   Strongly disagree

18. The Check Is in the Mail

The company's cash flow will not allow the controller to meet all the month's obligations. To handle the shortfall, he decides to mail the checks anyway, believing the "float" will cover the difference.

Strongly agree   1   2   3   4   5   Strongly disagree

19. That's Production's Problem

Deliveries are out six weeks. A salesperson has an opportunity to sell a large order if production can ship in four weeks. The sales manager says, "Let production worry about it. Give a four-week delivery, and get the order."

Strongly agree   1   2   3   4   5   Strongly disagree

20. We're Contractors, Not Preachers

The building inspector informs a construction manager that his nearly completed construction project is in violation of city codes. The inspector tells the manager that he realizes the company has a significant investment in the project at this point, and he will assist them in gaining approval if they pay him a consulting fee. After a series of meetings, the manager decides to pay the fee.

Strongly agree   1   2   3   4   5   Strongly disagree

21. Sell What We Have, Not What the Customer Needs

The company's product didn't quite fit the customer's requirements, so the salesman recommended a competitor's model. When the president learned how the situation was handled, he called the salesman and said, "If we lose this customer to our competitor because of this, you're fired."

Strongly agree   1   2   3   4   5   Strongly disagree

129

22. Seller Beware

A developer is considering purchasing three identical parcels of land for a shopping mall site. The land acquisition budget is $300,000. Two of the parcels are owned by investors and will cost $110,000 each. An uninformed farmer who is asking only $50,000 owns the third. Although there is no difference in the properties, it will exceed the budget to pay the farmer the same as the investors. As the prices are confidential, the developer decides to pay the farmer what he is asking.

Strongly agree   1   2   3   4   5   Strongly disagree

23. You Get What You Pay For

To sway a customer to award an order to your company, your salesperson hints that the competitor's product might be cheaper because it is made of inferior materials.

Strongly agree   1   2   3   4   5   Strongly disagree

24. We Bought It; We Can Do What We Want

Your office tries out a new piece of software. Others in the office like it and load the software on their computers, using the same single-user license.

Strongly agree   1   2   3   4   5   Strongly disagree

The Answers

The panel of judges (verification committee) selected to evaluate the questionnaire *strongly disagreed* with the action taken in *all* of the vignettes.

These vignettes correlated to the ethical principles as follows:

Principle	Questions
Don't steal	1, 3, 6, 17, 20, 24
Don't covet	4, 5, 9, 19, 21, 22
Don't deceive	7, 8, 10, 11, 13, 14
Don't mistreat others	2, 12, 15, 16, 18, 23

Surprisingly, some of the vignettes that made the final questionnaire were not the ones that I would have picked. Also, they were not categorized by the moral principle I would have selected. Certainly, some of the situations involve more than one principle, but our verification committee, created to pretest and certify the validity of the test, chose the scenarios and identified the ethics each violated. Maybe that says something about *my* value system?

Interestingly, although corporate America viewed stealing as the *most* serious unethical behavior, less than one-third of the executives we surveyed agreed with the unethical actions relating to stealing. Coveting was viewed as the *least* serious; over half agreed with the unethical actions relating to this principle.

Summary

Everyone has a set of ethics, but ethics vary with the individual and differ, to some degree, from the norm of society. In business, as well as in our personal lives, this variation has consequences. My research revealed that *coveting* was generally accepted among corporate executives. This might be anticipated since *coveting* is a vague act and harder to identify. However, the vignettes

131

that related to this behavior were specific, and the study also found that the participants were aware that it is unethical. *Stealing,* considered unethical by most of management, was the least abused; only one-third of those surveyed agreed with the behavior dealing with this issue. The behaviors, demonstrated by the vignettes, relating to *mistreating others* and *deceiving* were considered unethical about 50 percent of the time.

Obviously, as the results of the survey show, there is room for improvement in corporate ethics. However, since companies that improve their ethics also improve their profits, this also means that the bottom line can be improved in companies that are willing to make the effort. Of course, as with any successful program, it must be initiated and implemented by top management.

10

RECALIBRATING
YOUR MORAL COMPASS

*You can't learn too soon that the most useful
thing about a principle is that it can always
be sacrificed to expedience.*

W. Somerset Maugham

The four ethical principles—don't deceive, don't steal, don't covet, and treat others as you would want them to treat you—certainly won't cover every situation you will encounter in your career. They will, however, provide a moral bedrock on which to anchor your values. When the storms of business come, *and they will come,* you and your organization will be able to ride them out because your ethical foundation is solid. You will experience greater peace, security, and, as research indicates, higher profits.

Now that you've read how others in the corporate world related to these four principles, and perhaps you've taken the questionnaire and discovered how you viewed the vignettes, let's analyze them, using some real-world examples. Understanding how these principles apply to business is the first step in recalibrating your moral compass to the true north, the direction that leads to personal and professional dividends.

Deceiving

How can I trust a man not to lie when I would lie in his place?

Willard Butcher[1]

Vignette 14, "It's Standard Procedure," concerns an automobile dealership adding hidden fees. Adding fees not revealed in the negotiations is probably the most common of the six scenarios dealing with deception. Most of us have experienced this practice in some form or another. Most of us have bought a big-ticket item and found that the final bill was much larger than we anticipated. Certainly, some of the added taxes and fees are legitimate, but some are not.

My point is not that you need to challenge every charge and fee you don't understand or hadn't agreed to (although I would highly recommend this practice). My point *is* that we shouldn't have to. If we don't deceive each other in our business dealings, then we won't have to question everything about those exchanges.

We couldn't conduct business if we didn't have a reasonable expectation that the people with whom we were doing business were honest and were not out to deceive

134

us. We couldn't sell or buy our products and services without having a battery of attorneys drawing up contracts and making sure that every *i* was dotted and every *t* crossed. There wouldn't be enough courts in the land to handle all the suits brought as a result of breach of contract. Have you noticed how the volume of lawsuits has increased in the past thirty years?

Immanuel Kant, the eighteenth-century philosopher, asked, "What would happen if lying were generally accepted? What would happen if it were an everyday . . . practice of the business world that one person would borrow money from another with no intention whatever of repaying the loan?"[2] His answer, of course, was that conducting business would be impossible. I would add that civilized life as we know it could not exist.

The opposite course is to be truthful and honest in all of your dealings. "Let your 'yes' be yes and your 'no' be no," and over the long run, this will contribute to your success. It takes a while for people to develop a level of trust, to believe what you say. It doesn't happen overnight. We are by nature skeptical, and for good reason; we've all been burned. However, once you gain a reputation for being honest and fair, it's worth a lot.

I have been doing business with Moody's Tire & Auto Service in Franklin, Tennessee, for at least fifteen years. At first, I questioned everything they did, but over the years, they proved to be trustworthy and reliable. Their prices are fair, but more importantly, I can depend on them to maintain my car and not take advantage of my ignorance of automobiles. Yes, Jim Moody has made a few mistakes during our relationship. But the few times he turned out to be wrong, he made things right, and I never doubted his sincerity or honesty. The bottom line is, I trust him. I won't even consider taking my automobiles to someone else. There aren't enough advertising dollars in the world to buy this kind of loyalty. I can't

135

overemphasize this basic truth: people do business with people they trust.

Stealing

"I don't understand," asks the accountant. "If you are selling these copiers way under cost, how are you showing a profit?" "Simple," was the reply, "we make money by fixing them."

Unknown

Stealing involves more than taking something without permission. Taking supplies for personal use, making personal phone calls on company time, and padding your expense account all are stealing. Also, withholding something that belongs to someone else without that person's permission falls under this heading. I love the story about the lady who sent a check to the IRS for three hundred dollars with a note reading, "I cheated on my income tax and haven't been able to sleep since. This check covers half of what I owe. If I continue having trouble sleeping, I'll send the other half." We can all identify with the woman because of the way the government wastes our money. However, she is stealing from you and me because we have to make up the difference with higher taxes.

Unlike this woman, I don't cheat on my taxes. However, I really don't like sending my money to the IRS, not because I disagree with the philosophy of taxation, but because I believe a significant portion of what I send will be wasted on nonessential and ineffective programs. Some programs are simply ill conceived. But even if they

136

are well intended, by the time most have gone though the House and Senate and have been signed by the president, they have been so altered by compromise to special interests or have had so many amendments attached, that they no longer accomplish what they were originally designed for. In my opinion, this also is stealing. It's diverting our taxes into programs that benefit special interests.

Raising the price because of a special demand, the unethical behavior demonstrated in vignette 1, "Supply and Demand," is not an uncommon practice. My wife, Sonin, and I bought a Miata Limited Edition in 1992 when Miatas were hot. Only four thousand of these special cars were made that year. Because the demand was so great and the supply was exhausted, the dealer charged one thousand dollars more than the price another dealer had quoted me. The problem, of course, was the first dealer didn't have the car. Yes, I bought the Miata from the second dealer because he was the only game in town, but do you think I'll ever buy another car from him?

I have been involved in business activities for thirty-five years, and during that time, I know I've inadvertently done something similar to what this dealer did. I remember one situation where, although the price gouging wasn't as blatant, the results were the same. Business at my company was down; we needed sales. I had an opportunity to make a large sale if we would lower our price on a particular product. I made the decision to cut the price and get the order.

After the deal was consummated, Ned Jones, our marketing director, came into my office. He sat down, looked at me, smiled, and said, "Jerry, I understand why you lowered the price—we need the business; however, another customer who has ordered this same product

137

recently is paying a higher price. Is what we're doing ethical?"

Boy, did it hit me. I had been guilty of charging whatever the customer was willing to pay. Ned was gracious, as always, and encouraged me to do something I didn't want to do. I called W. T. Brogdon, my customer and my friend, and told him we were reducing the price and explained why. At the time, I felt like a fool, and I didn't think W. T. would understand. However, in hindsight, it was a good move, especially for the long haul. He may have been unsure of my motive at the time or thought we were stupid, but ultimately, he believed we were being honest and that we wouldn't take advantage of him in the future.

Coveting

You can't depend on your eyes when your imagination is out of focus.

Mark Twain

Coveting includes being selfish and having an unreasonable desire for something that doesn't belong to you. We all want things we don't have, but when this desire becomes unreasonable, or if in order to attain the object of our desire, we must harm someone else, then it is covetous.

Vignette 5, "The Insurance Dilemma," is a good example of this. The company management decided to drop the insurance and let the employees fend for themselves. They put profits before their employees. Of course, a company has to make a profit or it will go out of business. However, as I've emphasized, realizing

138

short-term profit at the expense of employees is not only unethical but can be poor business in the long run. When my company was facing this problem, we chose to continue to insure our employees even though profits would suffer (chapter 5). At the time, the decision was painful, but looking back, we really had no choice. If we wanted our people's loyalty, we had to take care of them during tough times. As it turned out, this decision eventually was profitable—for us and for the insurance company that took a chance on us because of our choice of people over profits.

As stated in chapter 3, a corporation has to make a profit or it will go out of business. Also the stockholders deserve a return on their investment. In vignette 9, "Image Is Everything," management expanded the company at the expense of (no pun intended) profits. This is a risky endeavor. If there are no profits, the growth has to be financed through debt, and there may not be resources to repay the debt. The company that inspired this vignette ultimately went under, and the stockholders lost their investment. This is okay if the investors are sophisticated, are aware of this risk, and approve of the program. However, in this case, it was a publicly held company, and the investors didn't know of the expansion plans until it was too late. Many people suffered because management coveted being an international company.

Treat Others As You Would Want Them to Treat You

Do not do unto others as you would have them do unto you. Their taste may not be the same.

George Bernard Shaw

The Golden Rule. Confucius advocated it, Jewish Rabbi Hillel advocated it, and Jesus advocated it: Treat others as you want them to treat you. It works in your personal life, and it will work in your business activities.

Vignette 18, "The Check Is in the Mail," dealt with floating checks. I suspect most of us have known someone who has done this, either in personal or business situations, or we have experienced it ourselves. When I first started my career, I worked for a company that not only floated checks but also mailed out unsigned checks. The vendor would then have to call, return the check, and wait for it to be mailed again. This would give the company an additional week of float. Fortunately, by the time I learned of the ploy, the company had been sold and the problem eliminated.

Remember the story of Lockheed Martin being offered insurance against a rocket launch failure? The company would get paid even if the rocket blew up on the launch pad. After a lot of soul searching, the chairman, Norman Augustine, chose not to take the insurance even though it made all the economic sense in the world, and Lockheed Martin had every legal right to do so. In this case, *you and I* are the customer. How do you feel about their decision? I don't know about you, but I want Lockheed Martin to share in the financial loss if there is an unsuccessful launch. I don't care how committed their engineers are. If it affects their wallets, then that's another strong incentive to make sure everything goes as planned. I applaud the management for their decision.

Isn't it interesting to compare Mr. Augustine's attitude to that of the Enron executives who negotiated plea agreements with federal prosecutors? Only when their assets were threatened and they were facing prosecution did they agree to turn state's evidence and testify to the corruption within the organization. Only when their backs were against the wall and it was in their best interest were they willing to do the right thing.

Summary

Are there moral absolutes that apply to business? Yes! Most of the ethical dilemmas faced by businesspeople can be addressed by these four principles:

1. Don't deceive. Don't misrepresent, withhold information, or give misleading information.
2. Don't covet. Coveting includes being selfish and having an unreasonable desire for something that doesn't belong to you.
3. Don't steal. Stealing includes theft, breach of contract (including verbal and implied contract), and lack of good faith effort.
4. Treat others as you would want them to treat you. This includes being fair, seeking justice, acting in good faith, and not using others.

My research indicates that adhering to these four principles will give you confidence in your judgment and decision making. Having a moral basis for making decisions will reduce stress and anxiety and promote peace and rest. It's no wonder my research found that managers become more ethical as they age. Older managers simply have had more experience with the consequences of good and bad judgment.

PART 4

THE HOLY GRAIL

Morality is a means to an end.

Happiness is that end.

Aristotle

11

ANATOMY
OF AN ETHICAL
CORPORATION

*You don't have to put greatness onto
people—you just have to elicit it, for the
greatness is already there.*

Billy Graham

Plato once said, "If you asked why we should educate someone, we educate them so that they become a good person, because good persons behave nobly." Other than the pragmatic benefits of staying out of jail or avoiding other direct consequences of bad behavior, why should anyone be good? Of what value are virtue, morality, and ethics? And is morality an end in itself or is it a means to an end? Well, my research indicates that,

145

to the virtuous person, ethical behavior is a means and, to the one receiving the virtuous action, an end. If a person's actions are directed at what he or she believes will ultimately bring him pleasure (utilitarianism), then doing good for others will eventually benefit them. It's the "what goes around, comes around" concept.

As I mentioned earlier, one of my most satisfying work environments was Rockwell Manufacturing's Power Tool Division in Jackson, Tennessee. Twenty-seven years later, I still remember it as one of the most pleasant experiences of my professional career. Why was it so gratifying? I have pondered this question and concluded it was due to the company's ethical attitude toward its employees, which provided the optimal structure for individual success. At Rockwell, I knew what was expected of me. The necessary resources were provided; Russ, my immediate supervisor, was always available to help and support me; and failure was accepted as a step toward success. Certainly, I had to perform my function or there would be consequences. But there were no unreasonable expectations, and I felt management was sincerely interested in *me*, not just in what I could produce. My time there was truly enjoyable and rewarding.

At the time, I was a product development engineer and could only see the organization from the inside out. Now I see the company from the outside in, affording me a clear view of the successes that have accrued to the corporation because of its principles. I believe Rockwell has over the years enjoyed the fruits Robert Krikorian defined in his remarks to the Tri-state Tax Conference in Milwaukee, Wisconsin:

- Satisfied, returning customers.
- Employees who are motivated, enthusiastic, supportive, and productive.

- A reputation for integrity and a credible voice.
- Reduced risk when faced with a crisis or catastrophe.
- Good relations with the community and the government.[1]

Tom Peters and R. H. Waterman, authors of *In Search of Excellence,* believe that companies that are excellently managed are value (virtue) driven. Read what they say about the importance of a strong value system:

It's not what happens to you that's important; it's how you deal with it that counts over the long haul.
Unknown

Every excellent company we studied is clear on what it stands for, and takes the process of value shaping seriously. In fact, we wonder whether it is possible to be an excellent company without clarity on values and without having the right sort of values . . . virtually all of the better performing companies we looked at . . . had a well defined set of guiding beliefs.[2]

Peters and Waterman built their careers by researching the benefits of a strong corporate value system. They have concluded it is foundational to long-term corporate success.

What kind of organization do you want to be affiliated with? One that has situational ethics that change according to the circumstances? One that believes every situation is different and ethics must be applied on a case-by-case basis? Do you want one that is primarily interested in how the bottom line affects management's pockets and whose management style reflects its self-centered perspective?

Or would you rather be associated with an organization that is committed to excellence? That requires all its members to perform excellently? One that has a written mission statement and a code of ethics and that holds itself accountable to them? One that takes into consideration the interest of all its stakeholders: stockholders, vendors, employees, and customers?

Would you prefer to belong to an organization that meets possibly unethical situations head-on and does the right thing, regardless of the consequences? Or one that does the expedient thing to make the situation go away, such as the computer company mentioned in chapter 2 that paid the foreign official even though the company had a policy against paying bribes. Sure, paying the bribe saved the day, but I wonder what it cost the company in the long run in employee respect and loyalty. Also, how many other companies have had to endure the same type of bribe because no one made the sacrifice, dug in, and fought the unscrupulous bureaucracy?

Obviously, we, as employees, would prefer to be with an organization that operates ethically. Well, organizations are just organized people. This means that companies shouldn't lie, cheat, steal, deceive, bribe, take bribes, or take advantage of employees any more than the people who operate them should. This may seem obvious, but when the pressure is on and a person's livelihood is on the line, the urge to do whatever it takes to succeed can be very powerful. Unless there are clear-cut codified principles and ethics to guide him, the line between ethical and unethical becomes blurred.

When the competition is trying everything to steal the business, the temptation to do unto others before they do unto you can be overwhelming, and doing what is right may not be at the top of the priority list. To combat this pressure, a set of values, such as the characteristics of an ethical person described in chapter 8, is needed to provide a basis for decisions. Rotary International has developed a "four-way code" as a guideline for business decisions, a code that businesses—and the individuals who make up those businesses—would do well to memorize:

1. Is it the truth?
2. Is it fair to all concerned?
3. Will it build good will and better friendships?
4. Will it be beneficial to all concerned?[3]

I can tell you from past experience that the old adage is true, "It's not what happens to you that's important; it's how you deal with it that counts over the long haul."

Codes of Ethics

One way to evaluate a company's commitment to excellence is to read their code of ethics. If they don't have one, it probably means they don't give ethics a high priority. If they do have one, then the question is, Do they live by it? If they do, then the question becomes, What does the code say about the organization? Let's consider the following:

Do Codes Work?

Yes, provided they are properly structured and implemented. A poorly drafted or executed code of ethics will have little effect on those who need guidance the most.

- Management, from the top down, must adhere to and enforce it.

- An ethics board must be established to review and enforce the code.
- The code is codified and disseminated in a way that is clear and can easily be followed.
- It supports, and is supported by, the mission statement.
- Employees must be thoroughly informed and committed.
- Management must walk the talk. Nothing undermines the effectiveness of an ethics program more than violations by top management.
- There is a mechanism for feedback and through which improvements can be made. People have different value systems, and they must have a forum to express their opinion and dialogue about things they disagree with or don't understand.
- A method of resolving ethical dilemmas is developed. Dilemmas *will* occur and must be resolved. If there isn't a formal, well-designed procedure in place, an informal one that at best is ineffective and at worst harmful will develop.

The Purpose of a Code of Ethics

- To promote law-abiding, safety-conscious, honest, and ethical employees, vendors, and other stakeholders.
- To give notice to outside interests that unethical relationships or behavior will not be tolerated.

The Benefits of a Code

- It provides a moral compass to employees. It's much easier for people to take the right stand if they understand the ethical principle involved, know the organization's position, and know that the right action—although it may be unpopular—will be supported.

- It improves the public image. People like to do business with people they trust.
- It improves the working environment for all stakeholders.
- It improves profits.

Components of a Good Code

- It defines the company's position on ethical issues.
- It promotes respect for the environment and the law, and good will toward all stakeholders.
- It places the needs of others above personal agendas.
- The benefits must extend to all shareholders.
- It promotes fairness and compassion.
- It defines remedies.
- It promotes integrity, respect, responsibility, and good citizenship.

A code of ethics provides written notice to all stakeholders defining how a corporation will conduct itself. I believe you cannot have a company that operates ethically unless management demands the organization abide by a solid code of ethics.

The Value of Effective Leadership

An organization is a living organism, constantly changing and growing in some direction. It also changes its personality and character to conform to changes in the personality and character of its leadership team. It

151

has been said, "If you want to see what kind of mate your significant other will make, look at the parents." If you want to see what kind of organization you are associated with, look at the leadership, primarily at the CEO. Study their personal beliefs, their value system, and what is truly important to them. Also, learn what plans and goals they have for the company and what strategies are being used to accomplish them. Is there a mission statement? What does it say? Is management committed to it, or do they just pay lip service? This is not to say that management is solely responsible for the ethical behavior of the entire organization, but through its policies, decisions, and actions, it establishes the moral environment, the corporate culture, to which the firm's other stakeholders generally conform. Principled leadership is the backbone of an ethical company.

You may remember a story about a coach in Virginia who locked the whole team out of the gym after some of the student athletes failed to meet the academic requirements of the school. There was an outcry from the parents of the other kids from the community who were locked out even though they met the requirements. Miraculously, after the team had forfeited several games, the deficient students' grades rose enough to meet the standards. When the coach was asked why he had punished the whole team, he responded, "In any organization, if some of the members fail to do their part, the whole team suffers. These kids need to learn that now." That, I believe, is leadership. The coach put the kids' welfare above winning.

I Don't Care How Much You Know Until I Know How Much You Care

What are the characteristics of an ethical leader? A leader, regardless of how intelligent or well trained, must

152

have strong core beliefs to be effective. I don't believe Richard Nixon would have lost the presidency if he had the character to do right when he first learned of the Watergate break-in; instead he employed situational ethics and did what was politically advantageous. He wasn't involved in the initial burglary. But when he learned of it, he opted for damage control instead of punishing the guilty. No organization is stronger than the character of its leadership, and a leader's character is no stronger than his core value system. Among the biblical proverbs left for our instruction and guidance, the author wrote these appropriate words: "When one rules over men in righteousness . . . he is like the light of morning at sunrise on a cloudless morning, like the brightness after rain that brings the grass from the earth."[4] The antithesis of this is, "There is a way that seems right to a man but in the end it leads to death."[5]

Although Peter Drucker, the management guru, has not (to my knowledge) conducted a statistically valid study on the benefits of ethics, his experiences and expertise qualify him to speak authoritatively on the subject. He believes that a person should not be in a position of responsibility if he or she is more interested in who is right than in what is right. "The final proof of the sincerity and seriousness of leadership is uncompromising emphasis on integrity of character," Drucker observed. He added that it is character through which leadership is exercised that sets the example, noting that coworkers, especially subordinates, quickly recognize whether or not someone has integrity. People need to believe that their superiors have their best interest at heart. Drucker concludes, "They may forgive a man (or woman) a great deal, incompetence, ignorance . . . but they will not forgive his lack of integrity."[6] Drucker recognizes a precept that must permeate an organization if it hopes to be successful.

153

Defining Leadership

When appraising leadership qualities, it is difficult not to evaluate people on appearance and personality. We are influenced by people's ability to impress us, by their charisma, and by their capacity to manipulate people. Although these are desirable characteristics for many careers, they are not the attributes that make successful leaders.

What qualities make leaders successful? We need to know where our leaders will take us, if they have the skills to get us there, and if they are the kind of people we want to follow. To find these things out, we must dig a lot deeper! To be an effective leader over the long haul, a person must have strong principles to draw on when faced with difficult decisions. The ethical characteristics leaders need in order to be successful include:

1. Reliability
2. Good judgment
3. Self-control
4. Loyalty
5. Stability
6. Vision
7. Love
8. Honesty
9. Integrity
10. Sincerity
11. Trustworthiness
12. Faith

By the time a person is mature enough to be in a leadership position, his or her value system is, for the most part, already formed. A fairly accurate picture of a person's character can be developed by looking at different areas of their life, seeing how they handle their affairs, and studying how they have performed in situations similar to the ones they are likely to encounter in their leadership position.

Reliability. Insight can be gained by studying a person's work history. How has he or she performed in the past? How consistent has this person been in their decisions? Can they be counted on to follow through with commitments?

Self-control. Is he or she given to overreacting under stressful situations? Do they have emotional outbursts? Are they cool and levelheaded under fire?

Stability. How dependable is he or she? Look at the number of positions this person has held in the last five to seven years. Frequent position changes may indicate instability.

Judgment. This will be reflected in the way they balance their responsibilities and activities. What are their priorities? Does this person make time for family, physical activity, and continuing education? What is his perspective toward life? Are they able to postpone gratification today if postponement is required to achieve long-term goals?

Vision. Do they have one? What is it? What are their personal goals, their family goals, and where do they plan to be five or ten years from now? Now the big question, What are this person's goals for the organization? Vision is an essential element of an ethical leader.

Love. What's love got to do with leadership? A lot! As the apostle Paul said in his letter to the Corinthians, "If I [can] speak in the language . . . of angels but have not love I am only a hollow noise."[7] In a sermon written from a jail cell, Dr. Martin Luther King wrote, "Love is the only force that is capable of transforming an enemy into a friend."[8] I would add, or a business adversary into an advocate. How does a leader love? By applying the Golden Rule. People don't care how much you know until they know how much you care. They will not follow a leader who doesn't care for them or who doesn't have their best interest at heart. If you want to see what kind of leader a person is, see what kinds of people follow that person.

Honesty. Show me a man or woman who is honest in small mundane things, and I will show you someone who is honest in big important things. Check with other business associates inside and outside the organization. How does this person conduct his business affairs? Does he conduct shoddy or under-the-table deals? Do others like transacting business with this person? Do they trust him? Would you trust him to look out for your interest?

Integrity, sincerity, and trustworthiness. These are interwoven and are foundational to a person's character. In order to evaluate these attributes, one must look at three things.

1. Family. Nothing reflects a person's character more than their attitude toward their spouse and children.
2. Religion and community organizations. Religious and organizational affiliations reveal volumes about a leader. What are his core beliefs and are they committed to those beliefs? What is his purpose for living? Does she have a relationship with a church or civic organization? What is her level of involvement? Where does this person spend his time when he isn't working?

3. Money. Show me a person's checkbook and I'll tell you where their heart is. Do they have financial goals? What is their attitude toward debt? Are they substantially in debt? How do they spend their money—big house, cars, expensive toys? Or are they frugal and manage their personal resources responsibly? Someone who can't manage their personal finances shouldn't be in charge of the organization's resources.

Loyalty. Other than integrity, there is no greater characteristic required of a leader than loyalty: loyalty to his team, to the other stakeholders, to the organization, and to his commitments. I know it sounds obvious, but it's so basic to human interaction. How can people follow someone who isn't loyal to them? Haven't we all known people who criticize another person behind his back or who agree when someone else is doing the denigrating? A leader should do the opposite; they should support the absent and characterize them in the best light possible.

Faith. It includes belief in the organization's mission and confidence in the team. How can one delegate without having faith in the people charged with the execution? Without faith, how can a leader reach beyond his grasp?

People are the only resource that really matters in an organization; without good people, the other resources cannot be employed effectively. And the leader determines whether the people are a team or a bunch of individuals. I don't care how good the leader is at administration if he or she doesn't possess most of the characteristics listed above. They can't lead or make hard decisions because

157

they don't have the bedrock principles to discern right from wrong, and they don't know where to go to find out.

Summary

What are the characteristics of a principled company? The ethical corporation should have a codified set of operating principles. It is value driven, and it conducts business by its operating principles. Its agenda is public, not hidden. It is consistent in applying its rules and fair and honest with all stakeholders. It has a good relationship with the community and enjoys a good reputation. Its employees are motivated. They have clear goals and operating instructions and are given the resources to perform their duties.

Ethical leaders embody the characteristics listed in this chapter. They are reliable, stable, and exhibit self-control. Their judgment is reflected in the way they balance their responsibilities and activities. Honesty, integrity, sincerity, and trustworthiness are at the core of their character. They are loyal. There is no greater characteristic (other than integrity) required of leaders than loyalty: to their team, to the other stakeholders, to the organization, and to their commitments. Ethical leaders must have faith in the organization's mission and in the team. And ethical leaders should love their organizations (the people) enough to put the organization's interest before the leader's own interest *but* not before their ethics.

Ethical leaders must have a vision. The vision is the picture of the organization after the leaders have met their goals. Without a clear picture of how the future organization will look, the stockholders, management, and employees can't know whether they want to be involved in creating this new entity. It is critical that leaders formulate a clear vision and articulate it to the members of the organization in such a way that they can make an informed decision.

The corporate organization is a living organism that is constantly growing and changing in some direction. It also changes its personality and character to conform to changes in the personality and character of its leadership team. A company is a team of individuals, and an ethical company must be comprised of ethical individuals, starting from the top down. An organization cannot be highly ethical if the leadership isn't.

12

SECURITY AND SIGNIFICANCE
The Holy Grail

Try not to be a man of success but rather a man of value.

Albert Einstein

So far, we've discussed the relationship between ethics and profits. Not only do ethics and profits coexist, but together they can make your business stronger. Also, we have identified the characteristics of an ethical organization and its leadership. Now let's focus on what's in it for you, the individual. Are there personal considerations that transcend your career as a corporate soldier?

James "Jimmy" West grew up in a home where achievement was important. His father placed significant value on success, especially in the business world. Although Bill West was never as successful as he would have liked, Jimmy and his sister learned at an early age that nothing would please their father more than accomplishing whatever they were engaged in.

Jimmy was successful at athletics, particularly baseball. He lettered in high school and won a scholarship to the University of Alabama. He also excelled in technical courses, such as computer science and other subjects that required deductive reasoning. However, he just couldn't seem to apply himself to courses that he wasn't interested in. Although there were bright spots in his academic career, overall he did poorly both in high school and college. He did, however, show an unusual aptitude for computers, and fortunately, the Internet was becoming the next gold rush.

After completing college, Jimmy signed with the Nashville Sounds, a minor league baseball team. For several years, he traveled the circuit playing second base, enjoying the notoriety and benefits of being a local celebrity. But after three seasons of hotels and cheap restaurants, the glitter was gone, and Jimmy decided it was time to "make something of himself," a phrase his father had been throwing at him for years. He quit the Sounds and began searching for a position that would allow him to use his aptitude for computers.

Jimmy did his research. He determined that the fastest way to achieve success would be to find a company that needed to be brought into the twenty-first century technologically. He took an entry-level position in an insurance company's computer networking department and began applying his considerable aptitude to improving the system. Almost immediately, he mastered his responsibilities and began asking for more. He excelled in everything he tried and was rapidly promoted. Within just a few months, he had acquired the necessary skills to perform any job in the department and soon found himself bored and looking around for another challenge.

A new career opportunity wasn't what he found. He discovered Kathy, a bright young claims adjuster who would also present him with a challenge. Jimmy redirected his focus and energy to "the Kathy project," as he called it. After weeks of relentless pursuing, his humor and wit won her over. She finally gave in and went out with him. They continued dating for several months, and as time passed, their affection for each other grew. For a time, they were satisfied to let nature take its course and just see where the relationship would go. Life was good—he had settled into a position that challenged him and still gave him time to court Kathy. However, after several months, Jimmy's computer skills had surpassed those needed for the company's requirements and he became bored.

Then Jimmy got a call. A large company on the West Coast needed someone with his skills to become a principal in a dotcom start-up. It was the opportunity he had been dreaming about. After two trips to California and a little research, he decided that if the venture were successful, it would make him a wealthy man. This was exactly what he wanted: a position where he could use his existing computer skills, grow and study the cutting-edge technology he really enjoyed, and get rich in the process. What a deal!

There was just one catch . . . the Kathy project. All of a sudden, the "let nature take its course" approach wasn't appropriate any longer, and a new game plan would have to be instituted. After days of reflection, soul searching, and sleepless nights, Jimmy decided he didn't want to go without her. They talked; she felt the same way, and he asked her to marry him.

It was a storybook engagement, marriage, and send-off. They took a train from Nashville to Los Angeles and spent the next two weeks honeymooning in Hollywood. They saw the sights by day and danced late into each night. They were in California to start a new life. Over the next two years, they did all the things newly married couples do. They rented an apartment, bought furniture, made friends, adopted a dog, and had Michael.

After a wild ride, the Internet stocks fell from favor on Wall Street, and as investment capital dried up, dot-com companies started folding. As Internet stocks plummeted and the prospect for a quick sale dimmed, Jimmy's dream of getting rich quick became less and less of a possibility. He dug in for the long haul. As the routine of life set in, Jimmy grew more like his father. He became involved in the company; and through his blood, sweat, and tears, the company started making money the old-fashioned way, by generating revenues and profits. As it grew, Jimmy took on more responsibility. His family would have to take a backseat for a while, just until he could get the company stabilized and generate enough revenues to hire adequate staff. "This shouldn't take long, maybe a year—two at the most," he thought.

Years passed. The company grew to almost a billion dollars in gross sales and had nineteen offices: four in South America, two in Japan, eight in Europe, and five in the States. Jimmy had a staff of five very capable managers and over fifteen hundred people under him. The growth was due, to a large degree, to Jimmy's hard work and perseverance.

He knew he had neglected his family. He had not been there for Kathy or to help raise Michael. He had missed his son's soccer games, school conferences, and several of his birthdays. Kathy had never forgiven him for refusing to fly home from England when she had to have an emergency appendectomy. He reasoned, "What can I do? I'm no doctor." He had worked so hard, had given up so much, and had been so successful; yet his desire to please his father was still unsatisfied—he still wasn't fulfilled. Maybe after the Colombia project was up and running, he would take some time off, reflect, and reconnect with Kathy and Michael.

The young man stuck his head through the door of the plush conference room and said in broken English, "Mr. West, your wife is on the phone." Jimmy was in a meeting with his South American management team discussing the available options for delivering entertainment over the Internet to the Bogotá, Colombia, residents. Things weren't going well. The cable infrastructure wasn't going to be completed for another two years and phone lines were too slow. However, the expense burn rate was up to $500,000 per month. He swore under his breath and said, "Now what?" Reluctantly, Jimmy picked up the phone. Between sobs Kathy said, "Jimmy, Michael was in an auto accident . . . he's . . . in the hospital . . . and the doctors don't expect him to make it. Please come home . . . I need you."

Jimmy's paradigm shifted. Suddenly, the delivery system wasn't important anymore. Colombia wasn't important. The company wasn't important. Jimmy went numb. No, this couldn't happen. Inadequacy and insecurity replaced confidence and self-reliance. In Jimmy's mind, Michael's face had replaced the burn rate. Now his priorities had changed. Now his wife and son were the truly important. He had to get home.

Sixteen-year-old Michael survived only eight days and never regained consciousness. Kathy was a basket case, not eating or sleeping. She just sat there looking at him, crying and wringing her hands. When he breathed his last breath, it was as if she breathed her last also. She just went dormant.

The funeral was awful. Jimmy went through the motions with the funeral director to make the arrangements, but he really didn't care. He knew Michael was a Christian and that he was with the Lord. The funeral was for the living and at that moment, he just didn't care about the living, just Kathy.

Kathy didn't seem to care about anything. She just sat and stared. She wouldn't eat, and when she was forced to go to bed, she would just lie there and stare at the ceiling. Jimmy would try to talk with her, comfort her, engage her, but she would only respond with, "I don't care," or "Whatever you want to do." They both were devastated, but Kathy turned inward, shutting Jimmy out. The worst part for Jimmy was that he never had a chance to tell Michael that he loved him.

Weeks passed. Kathy slowly pulled out of it, but there was something different. That spark of love that had been kept burning by Michael was gone. She was just a shell of a woman. She had no desire to do anything and no desire to be with or even talk to Jimmy. She really didn't seem to care if he was there or not. It was almost as if she didn't care if he existed. The common bond they had felt through Michael was gone, and the reality that Jimmy had left her emotionally years ago had now surfaced.

As for Jimmy, although he and Kathy stayed together, it was never the same. Michael was not there to provide a focus for their love. Jimmy went back to work and tried to engage himself in new projects, but the fire was gone. The thought of opening a new office, developing new software, or expanding into a new market—those things that had energized him in the past—just seemed empty and without any real value. He had learned, the hard way, that financial success is a poor substitute for love and the wonderful relationship between a husband and wife or between a father and son.

What do you really want out of life: more money, more prestige? Do you want a promotion, a larger house, luxury cars, an airplane, a boat? What really makes the hair on the back of your neck stand up or, put the way my friend Dr. John McDermit does, blows your hair back? While you are pondering this, consider how your priorities would change if you learned that one of your children had a terminal disease, with only a short time left to live, or if your spouse were in an accident and not expected to live. There is a real paradigm shift, isn't there? The big house and the boat aren't all that important, are they? Suddenly, other things that you have no influence over have reprioritized your life. Like Jimmy, you feel that you are being swept along by events you have no control over. Inadequacy and insecurity have replaced confidence and self-reliance, and disorder has replaced order and focus in your life. What I'm asking you to do is take time out and consider: What *is* truly important to you?

Measure wealth not by the things you have, but by the things you have for which you would not take money.
Anonymous

When it's all said and done, security and significance are what's truly important. They may mean different things to each of us, and we may search in different places for them, but these desires drive us to accomplish whatever we feel is necessary to achieve them. The problem is that we may be trying to achieve them by using the wrong methods. As the old adage goes, the success ladder we're climbing may be leaning against the wrong building. In order to understand the dynamics of the search for security and significance and how this relates to our business discussions, we need to depart from the realm of business for a moment and look inward to where we really live.

The Search for the Holy Grail

I'll have to admit I have my own struggle with the need for security and significance. I was born during the Great Depression, and early in my life, I was instilled with a scarcity mentality. Due to the circumstances I was raised in, I believed that there were insufficient resources to go around and that only through struggle and hard work could a person hope to provide enough to support a family. Although I now realize this isn't true—in America we don't have to work fourteen hours a day seven days a week—the feelings are still deep inside me. Because of my childhood experience, I believe that for some of us, our insecurities will never be healed, that the best we can do is recognize them for what they are and learn to live with them.

Security is knowing things are going to turn out okay; we have the resources to deal with whatever life throws at us. In this world, and particularly in the world of business, there are no guarantees that *anything* is going to turn out okay, so from where do you get your security? Oliver Wendell Holmes said, "What lies behind us and what lies before us are tiny matters compared to what lies within us." To fulfill this need, we must look within.

Until I was fifty-two years old, due to my childhood, my feelings of security were, to a large degree, derived from my business activities. As earlier stated, I'm a Christian, and my ultimate hope is in Jesus Christ. Also, my wife, Sonin, and my family are very important in my life. Christianity and family are where I applied my resources. But because of my childhood, my paradigm was that my security and significance were derived through work.

Oh sure, I daydreamed about the day I wouldn't have to work and could do other things, but that was someday. At the time, although it's embarrassing to admit, I

168

felt my value as a human being was determined by how well I provided for my family. My security and significance were intertwined with my ability to generate resources, and this colored my whole value system.

Then one of the priority-changing events that I talked about earlier happened. I had a heart attack. Fortunately, it was mild with no debilitating effect, but for four months after the attack, I sank into major depression from a chemical imbalance created by the trauma. This event and the ensuing depression dramatically changed my priorities. During my depressed stupor, the truth hit me: I wasn't going to live forever. For the first time in my life, I truly understood that I was mortal and was really going to die—sometime in the *not too distant* future. What about all of those things I said I wanted to do someday? Well, someday had arrived, and I had to rethink my priorities and get with the new program. Also, I finally realized I couldn't rely on my profession for my security and significance.

Don't misunderstand; I continue to struggle with security issues today. In fact, Sonin and my friends nicknamed me Captain Doom because my basic nature is to believe that disaster is just around the corner, and it's my job to worry about things because no one else can worry as well as I. Fortunately, I'm able to laugh at my insecurities and, through logic and reason, dismiss my bad feelings in light of the reality of the situation. However, I still keep a list of things to worry about in my mind's filing cabinet.

Don't Build Your Nest in the Wrong Tree

Security shouldn't come from our wealth, health, or relationships with other people. If we depend on these things, we *will* be disappointed. A friend (I'll call Don) once was working for a man (we'll call Bob) who was

169

gifted in business strategy. Bob could devise strategies that would work when all else failed. His real expertise lay in creating opportunities out of bad situations, and he was good at it. He was also amoral. He, like Dr. Carr, felt that business had its own set of rules that applied to the game of commerce (see p. 43).

Don was ethical but also loyal. He thought that because he was a team player that after he had voiced his opinion, he should support his boss. He didn't understand that he should place loyalty to his principles before loyalty to his supervisor. He also didn't understand that not everyone plays by the same rules.

When a deal the company was working on fell through and they were unable to pull it out of the fire, Bob (the boss) took it hard. He couldn't accept the failure and needed an excuse, a scapegoat. He laid the blame squarely at Don's feet, and as a result, my friend was asked to resign. Don was devastated emotionally and financially, but he later realized it was for the best. He had placed his security in his employer whom he trusted to have his best interest at heart. He learned a valuable lesson—not to put his security in other people.

Luke, Trust the Force

Dr. Stephen Covey used an exercise that communicates my message beautifully. Although I'm not going to quote him verbatim, the idea is his.[1] Find a comfortable isolated place where you won't be distracted until you finish doing this exercise. Clear your mind of the tyranny of the urgent and consider your death. Yes, your death. We all are going to die and probably untimely. (I don't know anyone who died a timely death.) But for this purpose, imagine that you will die three years from now. Think about it! You're at your own funeral; your friends, family, and business associates (some who care and some who just feel obligated) are there.

There is a minister conducting the service and, depending on your faith, some number of other people assisting him. Now imagine that three people are chosen to deliver the eulogy: one from your family, one from your friends, and one from your profession. Now consider what they would say about you. For what would they honor you: your big house, your fancy cars, how much wealth you have accumulated? Maybe secretly, you would like it known that you had been more successful than your high school friends. Would you want them to talk about how successful you had been in business? Remember Jimmy West? They could have gone on and on about his innovations and accomplishments in the Internet industry. Would you want to be compared to other great industry giants of your profession? All of us desire significance, don't we? But when your life is over, do you really want to be eulogized by your friends for your business achievements? Certainly not. Well, what *would* you want them to focus on? What attributes would you like them to talk about? What is truly important to you?

What I'm asking you to consider is, what would you want for your epitaph? If you could write the words that best described your achievements in this life, what one or two things are truly important enough to be put on your gravestone? What accomplishments are significant enough to you that you would want to be remembered for them? Well, these are the things you need to be investing your time and resources in now, while you can do something about your life, your eulogy, and affect the way you are remembered.

I believe high on your list of the things you hold dear and would want to be remembered for would include: being loving, having integrity (honesty, truthfulness, and reliability), and being generous. Also, being a person of

171

high morals and ethics whose life made a difference may come to mind. These are the attributes you should strive to inculcate. Acquiring these attributes produces security and significance.

Summary

I would challenge you to decide what you really want out of this life. What is truly important to you? What is it that will ultimately give you security and significance? If you haven't yet determined this, I would suggest you do the epitaph writing exercise that was discussed earlier in this chapter. Then develop a personal mission statement that includes a set of rules that you will live your life by, not only your professional life but also all facets of your life. It should include:

- The truly important, your priorities.
- The basic principles that will guide your decision-making process and underwrite your value system.
- How you will spend your time. We all have twenty-four hours a day, and it *will* be allotted some way.

Consider how you would like your epitaph to read and how you will have to live in order for it to be true. Then look at your activities to see if they contribute to what your mission statement says you are about. Realign your life so that you are investing your time and energy in worthwhile activities and projects that make a significant impact on your stated mission.

13

PEACE *AND* PROFIT
The Real Bottom Line

You aren't born with character; you learn it.

Unknown

When I was five, my uncle died, and his wife and four children moved in with us. Uncle Frank had been ill with tuberculosis for several years, and the disease had robbed the family of their financial resources and of his leadership. Times were tough; all of the adults worked, and we kids were left to ourselves most of the time. Although my parents and my older brother had good values, my value system was still being formed, and it developed primarily from interaction with my cousins. Together, my cousins and I developed our own code of ethics, one that *didn't* include, Do unto others as you would have them do unto you. Only later, after many mistakes that I still regret, did I take stock of myself and resolve to develop moral principles to guide my life, decisions, and goals. I began to move from reactive, situational ethics to proactive, principle-based decisions.

Yes, there are those of us who didn't learn good values as children and have had to struggle with right and wrong throughout our lives. Others, however, were fortunate enough to have been taught good morals early but later found themselves under pressure to violate their ethics. This is the case of the National Semiconductor employee, discussed in chapter 2, who, under pressure to do a good thing, allowed some government-required testing of military components to be omitted because the company couldn't keep up with demand. Over time, like the frog in hot water, he became more comfortable with the omissions. I'm sure that many of the people who are involved in the current scandals had no intention, initially, of involving themselves in the kind of unscrupulous activities they are now accused of. In the beginning, it just seemed like the best thing to do, and then they found themselves on the slippery slope.

Obviously, you can't go back and correct many of the actions you regret. However, you can take responsibility for future decisions and actions. When one decides to make the effort to develop and live by a set of ethical principles, he or she begins to enjoy physical, emotional, and intellectual benefits as well. Also, as a result of being more ethical, one experiences ethical reciprocity from those he or she associates with. A person who lives by convictions enjoys greater peace.

According to the *Wall Street Journal,* London House tested 111 executives, middle managers, and professionals to see if there was a relationship between their ethics and their well-being. The participants were asked whether they agreed or disagreed with unethical or illegal actions, and the answers were compared to their scores on hostility, anxiety, and fear. The consulting firm found a striking correlation. "The more emotionally healthy the executives, as measured on a battery of tests, the more likely they were to score high on the ethics test." The conclusion drawn from this study was that the more ethical the executive, the less likely he or she was to be anxious or fearful.

The process is progressive. As principles become ingrained by being tested over time, people gain confidence in their decision-making process and learn to rely on their value system. Using principles as a guide when faced with ethical dilemmas, they have a foundational "operating manual" to fall back on. As London House found, this reliance reduces stress and anxiety. Research has also shown that reducing stress promotes better sleep, better health, greater ability to fight illness, and ultimately, longer life.[1]

The Calm after the Storm

Interestingly, when wrestling with a thorny situation, the hardest part is defining the problem and the underlying principles involved. Once the issue is defined and the applicable principles are identified, the circumstances no longer weigh a person down. A decision can be made based on those principles, and the correct action can be taken with confidence. Then we can feel secure in having done our best and can rest emotionally, safe from doubt that the actions taken were correct and free of fear that a mistake might have been made. A sense of peace and contentment replaces worry and self-distrust. I love the statement in Proverbs where Solomon, one of the wisest and richest men who ever

175

lived, discussed the benefits of wisdom (principles): "This will bring health to your body and nourishment to your bones."[2]

In chapter 5, we discussed a situation where my company was faced with a health insurance dilemma that required management to decide between losing income at a time when the company could ill afford losses or not providing insurance for its employees. I was involved in that decision, and I can tell you that once the decision was made, based on the company's philosophy "to make short-term decisions that make the most long-term sense," we could all sleep better. We knew that we had done the right thing, regardless of the outcome. As Solomon also said, "The righteous [ethical] man is rescued from trouble."[3]

Principles Are Better than Steroids

Confidence builds strength, and confidence comes from believing one has the resources to deal with a situation. But what about situations where the resources just aren't available or when it's unclear what resources are required? We have all faced circumstances where there just didn't seem to be a clear right choice. My advice, in these situations, get counsel! Proverbs 11:14 states, "Many advisers make victory sure," and Proverbs 1:5 says, "Let the wise listen and add to their learning, and let the discerning get guidance." When we talk through the issues with men and women who have integrity and experience, the real problem will surface and clarity will replace uncertainty. Then one's principles can be accessed to provide a foundation on which to base decisions and strategies. Once the foundational principles that apply to the circumstances are identified, then the decision process can proceed in an orderly fashion, restoring confidence.

The decision maker then has an understanding of the situation and how it relates to the big picture. He or she becomes wise in the use of the available information and can separate the truly important from the urgent. A person with the ability to accurately evaluate the principles underlying a situation can operate at a higher level of efficiency with less uncertainty. Order replaces frustration, actions can be initiated, and the situation can be put to rest.

If I take care of my character, my reputation will take care of itself.

Dwight Moody

This philosophy is embodied in Dr. Peter Drucker's statements regarding the workplace of the future. He contends that the leader must be grounded in and operate from the "bedrock" of principles, "that he lead not only through knowledge, competence, and skill but through vision, courage, responsibility, and integrity."[4]

Imagine what our professional lives would be like if there were no underlying standards of honesty among businessmen and women? Chaos would reign. Some level of integrity has to exist in order to conduct business. When you make an appointment with someone, you expect that person to show up. When someone says he will purchase a product or service from you over the phone, you should have a reasonable expectation that he will follow through. We take for granted that people will act according to a code of ethics.

Over a period of time and multiple transactions, we either gain a reputation for having integrity and honesty or become known as dishonest and untrustworthy. People relate to a person based on the relationship developed from past transactions and the reactions of others.

As I have said before, people like doing business with people they trust. Truthfulness and integrity are valued

177

by everyone, even dishonest people, but even more so by people who have high moral standards themselves. A person with a good reputation is respected; others want to associate with him and want to help him succeed. Honesty and integrity actually protect a person because they encourage others to act honestly and ethically toward him. Anyone can be taken advantage of by an unscrupulous person or be blindsided by an unforeseen disaster. But the risk is greatly reduced if other people like and respect someone. They become genuinely interested in his well-being and are willing to inform him of potential pitfalls. Over the long run, statistics and odds come into play, and the chances of success are enhanced because people are looking out for him.

Am I My Brother's Keeper?

One of the basic principles in a moral foundation is an extension of the Golden Rule; if you want true success in your relationships and a good reputation, take good care of your brother. Martin Niemoller offers this insight from the Holocaust of World War II:

> When they came for the Catholics, I didn't protest because I'm not a Catholic. When they came for the Polish, I didn't protest because I'm not Polish. When they came for the Blacks, I didn't protest because I'm not Black. When they came for the Jews, I didn't protest because I'm not Jewish. When they came for me, there was no one left to protest.[5]

Yes, you are your brother's keeper. If you don't keep your brother, who will? As Jesus said: "Do to others what you would have them do to you."[6] In the language of business, Jesus was saying to put other stakeholders' interests ahead of your own. Who is your brother? In business, he is your customer, your coworker, your supplier, your community, and your stockholder. Also, in some cases, he's your competitor.

Your brother the customer: Don't just sell him a product or service; instead, take time to learn about that customer's needs. Then do your best to meet those needs, even if it means sending the customer to a competitor. Be trustworthy; do what you say you will, and don't promise more than you can deliver, whether in product, service, or delivery.

Your brother the coworker: Develop an honest, truthful working relationship. Dr. Covey coined a term, "Emotional Bank Account."[7] It's a metaphor that describes the amount of trust built up between two people. If the account is low, there is suspicion and low trust. However, if there has been a strong trusting relationship and the emotional bank account is full, then even when one makes a mistake and does something that harms the other person, communication is easy, and the problem can be resolved. Keep the emotional bank account full.

There is a term seldom used in business discussions, primarily because it has other connotations such as romantic: love. Yes, love your coworker. I'm not talking about romantic love, but the same kind of love you have for your family and friends. The apostle Paul wrote:

Love is very patient and kind, never jealous or envious, never boastful or proud, never haughty or selfish or rude. Love does not demand its own way. It is not irritable or touchy. It does not hold grudges and will hardly even notice when others do it wrong. It is never glad about injustice, but rejoices whenever truth wins out. When you love someone, you will always believe in him, always expect the best of him, and always stand your ground in defending him.[8]

179

This is the attitude I'm advocating. Practice this attitude, and live in peace with your coworkers. You'll sleep better.

Your brother the supplier: Treat him the same way you treat your coworkers because that is what they are; you're in business together. I just finished reading a book on business where the author advocated stretching out payables. "Don't pay the invoice until the supplier calls twice," he warned.

I'm sure this delay tactic will improve the cash flow for a time, but it's been my experience as a vendor that the supplier will either raise the future price to compensate for the late payment or stop doing business with the customer. This strategy won't work over the long haul, and it's just not the right thing to do. At the very least, it damages the business relationship by creating distrust and suspicion. We owe our brother, in this case the vendor, honesty.

When we order goods or services, we agree to pay within certain terms, and if it's within our ability to pay, we should do so. If we can't pay, then we should go to the vendor and tell him the truth. In my business, over fifty cents of my sales dollar goes to pay for material and supplies. Our vendors are in a position to make or break our company, and I want them rooting for us, not pulling against us. Do it because it's good business and because it's the right thing to do.

Your brother the stockholder: Do your best to produce a fair return on his investment and minimize his risk. How do you do this? By practicing the virtues discussed above. Managing the company's activities in this way will provide stability and promote good will from other businesses and from the community. It doesn't take a rocket scientist to know you'll sleep better if your stockholders are happy.

Your brother the competitor: Most businesspeople think of their competition as the enemy. He is the guy that is trying to take your business away any way he can. I used to feel the same way. But during an industry conference, I had the opportunity to meet some of my competition. After sitting down with them and discussing common problems, I got to know some of them. You know, they weren't bad people. Yes, some competitors are unethical—every industry has its share—but most are honest, hardworking men and women just trying to carve out a living the best way they know how. You owe your competition a level of professional courtesy. This means:

- Treat them with respect when discussing them with the customer.
- Don't criticize or lie about their products and services.
- If you can't satisfy the customer's needs, send him to your competition who can.

It means treating them the way you want to be treated.

Most of us spend between one-third and one-half of our waking life involved in our occupation. This time and energy should be spent in engaging in meaningful relationships, working toward meaningful goals, and living by our principles just as we do when we are in church or involved in other areas of our life. Indeed, there should be no distinction between the way we conduct our business life and our personal life.

No Man (or Company) Is an Island

In our capitalistic society, business is one of the most dominating forces, and what we do in our business activities flows over into our personal lives. Corporate America is the source of our country's wealth. It provides our goods and services, funds universities and basic research, and, through advertising, it also funds our entertainment. It wields a big stick. But companies are essentially collections of individuals. They are made up of people just like you and me, and, just as raindrops make rivers, it is people's attitudes toward the conduct and actions of businesses that determine the moral direction of corporate America.

Ethics are not only a list of dos and don'ts; they also include policies that promote the Golden Rule among all stakeholders. They require internal policies that include treating employees with respect, being honest with them, and empowering them. They entail external policies that mandate working with customers and suppliers, encouraging teamwork, and doing what you promised. Fulfilling the moral obligation of responsible corporate citizenship in communities at home and in other countries is another ethical directive. As stated earlier, Levi Strauss dropped 5 percent of its contractors and mandated improvements in another 25 percent to insure that acceptable human rights practices were followed in undeveloped countries.[9]

Isaac Newton discovered the physical law dictating that for every action there is an equal and opposite reaction. I believe this law can be applied to the social sciences, and that you and I as employees and managers must supply that moral action. My research in business ethics found a correlation between ethics and profits: ethical actions bring ethical (and profitable) reactions. An organization that incorporates ethics into every facet of its activities will accrue these benefits. A company that truly operates by ethical principles is more profitable, more successful, and more stable. It is a happier, more peaceful place to work and provides better benefits. It is more effective in the utilization of its resources. It is more

182

respected in the community, and its employees are better citizens, better spouses, and better parents.

Summary

Establish fundamental principles that will stand the tests of fire and time and by which all the strategies and tactics of life can be judged. Make this set of basic operating principles a part of your personality and character. Refer to them often and refine them. Even if you may not have been taught good values as a child, over time, if you reflect on them and adhere to them, they will become a part of your personality. One very good source of ethical principles that I use and highly recommend is the Book of Proverbs. Solomon, one of the wisest men and the richest man who ever lived, wrote most of the proverbs over twenty-seven hundred years ago, and they have stood the test of time.

All of us want to know that our actions touch others in a positive way and that while working toward worthwhile goals, we are creating a better place for others. Developing and adhering to foundational ethical principles will give you confidence that your decisions are right, and you will sleep well knowing that you are living according to your deep beliefs. In changing your paradigm, you will change *your* world, and according to the social application of Newton's law, you will change the world.

NOTES

Chapter 1 Enron

1. Susan Orenstein, "The Last of the True Believers," *Business 2.0* (March 2002): 21.

2. Marie Brenner, "The Enron Wars," *Vanity Fair* (April 2002): 206.

3. Ibid., 196.

4. Ibid., 182–84.

5. David S. Hilzinrath. January 22, 2002. "Fired Auditor Says Enron, Arthur Anderson [sic] Share the Blame," http://www.Polkon line.com/stories/012202/bus_auditor.shtml [January 22, 2002].

6. Wilson Siu. February 6, 2002. "Avoiding another 'Enron,'" *University Wire*, http://www.elibrary.com [March 28, 2002].

7. Allan Sloan, "Who Killed Enron?" *Newsweek*, January 21, 2002, 19–20.

8. Brenner, "Enron Wars," 184.

9. Brooks Jackson. January 14, 2002. "Enron Employees Ride Stock to Bottom," http://www.cnn.com/law/01/14/enron.employ ees/index.html [March 21, 2002].

10. Brenner, "Enron Wars," 186.

11. Siu, "Avoiding another 'Enron.'"

12. March 8, 2002. "Bush: Crackdown on Corporate CEOs," *White House Fact Policy Statement*. http://usgovinfo.about.com/library/ weekly/aa030802a.htm [March 28, 2002].

Chapter 2 Is the System Flawed?

1. Laura L. Nash, *Good Intentions Aside: A Manager's Guide to Resolving Ethical Problems* (Boston: Harvard Business School Press, 1990), 1.

2. Robert C. Solomon, *It's Good Business* (New York: Athenaeum, 1985), 25.

3. Andrew Singer, "Can a Company Be Too Ethical?" *Across the Board* 30 (April 1993): 20.

4. David Williams and David Sylvester, "How Tests Were Faked at National," *San Jose Mercury News*, June 3, 1984, sec. 12A.

5. Albert Z. Carr, "Is Business Bluffing Ethical?" *Harvard Business Review* (1968): 67.

6. Solomon, *It's Good Business*, 37.

7. William Lawrence and Jack Turpin, *Beyond the Bottom Line* (Chicago: Moody Press, 1994), 15.

8. Milton Friedman, *Capitalism and Freedom* (Chicago: Moody Press, 1978), 15.

9. Dirk J. Struik, *Birth of the Communist Manifesto* (New York: International Publishers, 1971), 106.

10. Ralph Nader, Mark Green, and Joel Seligman, *Taming the Giant Corporation* (New York: W.W. Norton, 1976), 29.

11. Ibid.

Chapter 3 Profit Is Not a Dirty Word

1. Jonathan Lieberson, "Harvard's Nozick: Philosopher of the New Right," *New York Times Biographical Service* (December 1978): 1235.

2. Solomon, *It's Good Business*, 25.

3. R. C. Sproul, *Ethics and the Christian* (Wheaton: Tyndale, 1983), 59.

4. Douglas A. Blackmon, Martha Brannigan, Glenn Burkins, and Laura Jereski, "The UPS Strike—What the Sides Wanted and What They Got," *Wall Street Journal*, August 19, 1997, sec. A5.

5. Adam Smith, *The Wealth of Nations*, books I-III, ed. Andrew Skinner (Hamondsworth, Middlesex, England: Penguin, 1974), 136.

6. Peter F. Drucker, *Management* (New York: Harper & Row, 1985), 40.

7. Matthew 25:14–27 TLB.

8. John Stieber, *The Role of Profit* (Boston: Warren, Gorham, & Lamont, 1987), 8.

Chapter 4 Being Ethical Isn't Profitable . . . or Is It?

1. Quoted in J. I. Merritt, "Automakers Eye Durbin Engine Design," *Princeton Parent News* (February 1, 1980): 1.
2. Singer, "Can a Company Be Too Ethical?" 1.
3. Ibid.
4. Ibid., 9.
5. Ibid., 16.
6. Ibid., 5.
7. Ibid., 4.
8. Thomas Shanks. 2001. "The Case of Due Diligence," Markkula Center for Applied Ethics, Santa Clara University. http://www.scu.edu/ethics [November 22, 2002].
9. Singer, "Can a Company Be Too Ethical?" 1.
10. Ibid., 2.
11. Nash, *Good Intentions Aside*, 32.
12. Edmond P. Learned, Arch Dooley, and Robert L. Katz, "Personal Values and Business Decisions," *Harvard Business Review* (March/April 1959): 86.
13. Jagannath Dubashi, "God Is My Reference Point," *Financial World* (fall 1994): 36.
14. Walter Thomas, "Relationships among Business Ethics, Religion, and Organizational Performance" (Ph.D. diss., Georgia State University, 1990), 95.
15. S. D. Lydenberg, A. T. Marlin, S. O. Stubbs, and the Council on Economic Priorities, *Rating America's Corporate Conscience* (Boston: Addison-Wesley, 1986), 12.
16. James Burke, address to the Advertising Council, New York, December 16, 1983.
17. Thomas, "Relationships among Business Ethics, Religion, and Organizational Performance," 44.
18. "Ethics in American Business: A Special Report." (New York: Touche Ross, 1988), 69.
19. Louis H. Grossman, "A Study of Eight New York Exchange Industrials Which Have Paid Dividends for 100 Years or More" (Ph.D. diss., Arizona State University, 1982), 22.
20. M. Zetlin, "Ethics and Common Sense," *Management Review* (1991): 59.
21. S. M. Rao and J. B. Hamilton III, "The Effect of Published Reports of Unethical Conduct on Stock Prices," *Journal of Business Ethics* 15 (1996): 1321–30.

Chapter 6 The Good, the Bad, and the Ugly

1. Frank Navran. March 26, 1998. "The Costs of Unethical Behavior," The Ethics Resource Center. http://www.ethics.org [March 25, 1998].
2. Nash, *Good Intentions Aside*, 9.
3. Patrick Primeauz and John Stieber, "Profit Maximization: The Ethical Mandate of Business," *Journal of Business Ethics* (April 1994): 291–92.
4. Marc Gunther, "Yikes, Diane Sawyer's Downstairs!," *Fortune* 134 (December 23, 1996): 231.
5. Scott Andron, "Scratch Car Saves ABC," *Quill Magazine* (September 1997).
6. "Workers Pressured to Ignore Violations," *USA Today* (August 1995): 4.
7. Marian M. Jones, "In Bad Company," *Psychology Today* (July/August 1997): 20.
8. Francis J. Aguilar, *Managing Corporate Ethics* (New York: Oxford University Press, 1994), 7–13.
9. Thomas Eggleston. "Driver's Mart Dealer Participation Information." http://www.drivsmart.com [April 3, 1998].
10. Karen Aylsworth, "Inside Track: Thomas Eggleston," *Grand Rapids Business Journal* 15, no. 34 (August 25, 1997): 5–6.
11. Psalm 73:13–14, 18–20 TLB.

Chapter 7 I'm Ethical . . . Right?

1. James Patterson and Peter Kim, *The Day America Told the Truth* (New York: Prentice-Hall, 1990), 65.
2. Michael Quinn, "It's All in the Lie: Cheats on the Links Are Cheats on the Job," *Time* (July 26, 1993): 54.
3. Ralph Linton, "Cultural Relativity," mimeographed report given at Swarthmore College under auspices of the Cooper Foundation (October 1951).
4. C. S. Lewis, *The Case for Christianity* (New York: Macmillan, 1946), 5–7.
5. "American State Papers: John Stuart Mill," in *Great Books of the Western World*, vol. 43, ed. Robert Maynard Hutchins (Chicago: Encyclopædia Britannica, 1952), 448.
6. W. T. Stace, *The Concept of Morals* (New York: Macmillan,1962), 104.
7. Bernard Gert, *The Moral Rules* (New York: Harper Torchbooks, 1966), 66.

8. Richard B. Brandt, *Ethical Theory: The Problems of Normative and Critical Ethics* (Englewood Cliffs, N.J.: Prentice-Hall, 1959), 121–31.

Chapter 8 Are There Absolutes? Absolutely!

1. Rushworth M. Kidder, *Shared Values in a Troubled World* (San Francisco: Jossey-Bass, 1994), 18.
2. Hans Kung, *Global Responsibility* (New York: Crossroad, 1991), 57.
3. Confucius, as quoted in "The Golden Rule." http://www.fragrant.demon.co.uk/golden.html. [December 4, 2002].
4. I. Kant, *Fundamental Principles of the Metaphysics of Ethics.* http://www.epistemelinks.com/Main?Quotations.aspx?PhilCode=Kant. [December 4, 2002].
5. B. A. Robinson. "Shared Beliefs in the Golden Rule: Ethics of Reciprocity." Samyutta Nlkaya v. 353. http://religioustolerance.org/reciproc.htm [November 22, 2002].
6. Ibid., "Shared Beliefs in the Golden Rule." Mahabharata, 5:1517.
7. Ibid., "Shared Beliefs in the Golden Rule." Forth Hadith of an-Nawawi, 13.
8. Ibid., "Shared Beliefs in the Golden Rule." Rabbi Hillel, 60 BCE–10 CE.
9. Matthew 7:12.
10. Exodus 20:1–17 and Matthew 7:12.
11. David Ross, *Aristotle, Nichomachean Ethics*, bk. I (London: Oxford University Press, 1998), 343.
12. Stephen R. Covey, *Principle Centered Leadership* (New York: Summit, 1990), 33–39.
13. Raymond Baumhart, *An Honest Profit* (New York: Holt, Rinehart and Winston, 1968), 50–54.
14. Peter F. Drucker, *Management: Tasks, Responsibilities and Practices* (New York: Harper & Row, 1993), 368.
15. Charles Colson, "The Problem of Ethics." Speech presented to Harvard Business School, April 4, 1991.

Chapter 9 I Wish Everyone Were As Righteous As I

1. Nash, *Good Intentions Aside*, 9.

Chapter 10 Recalibrating Your Moral Compass

1. Willard Butcher, "The Need for Ethical Leadership," *Ethical Speeches* (August/September 1994): 28.
2. Tom L. Beauchamp and Norman E. Bowie, eds. *Ethical Theory and Business.* Englewood Cliffs, N.J.: Prentice-Hall, 1993), 36.

Chapter 11 Anatomy of an Ethical Corporation

1. Robert V. Krikorian, "Ethical Conduct and the Bottom Line," *Executive Speeches* (August/September 1994): 48.
2. Thomas J. Peters and Robert H. Waterman Jr., *In Search of Excellence* (New York: Harper & Row, 1982), 280–81.
3. Rotary International's "Four Way Code." http://www.official products.com/rotary.htm
4. 2 Samuel 23:3–4.
5. Proverbs 14:12.
6. Drucker, *Management*, 462.
7. 1 Corinthians 13:1–2 TLB.
8. Martin Luther King Jr., *Strength to Love* (Philadelphia: Fortress, 1981), 47.

Chapter 12 Security and Significance

1. Stephen R. Covey, *Seven Habits of Highly Effective People* (New York: Simon & Schuster, 1989), 96.

Chapter 13 Peace *and* Profit

1. Amanda Bennett, "Unethical Behavior, Stress Appear Linked," *Wall Street Journal,* April 11, 1991, sec. B1.
2. Proverbs 3:8.
3. Proverbs 11:8.
4. Drucker, *Management*, 378.
5. Martin Niemoller, "Stuttgart Statement of Guilt," *Philosophical Library Publications* (1945).
6. Matthew 7:12.
7. Covey, *Seven Habits of Highly Effective People*, 188.
8. 1 Corinthians 13:4–7 TLB.
9. Thomas Donaldson, "Values in Tension," *Harvard Business Review* 74, no. 5 (September/October 1996): 48–56.

Dr. Jerry W. Fleming has served as Chief Executive Officer for three companies. He earned his doctorate from Oxford Graduate School in Dayton, Tennessee, where he wrote his dissertation on the relationship between morality and the earnings of publicly held companies. He and his wife, Sonin, live in Sanibel Island, Florida.